ORIENTAL BANQUETS

CHARMAINE SOLOMON

HAMLYN

Published 1993 by Hamlyn Australia,
an imprint of the Octopus Publishing Group,
a division of Reed International Books Australia Pty Ltd
22 Salmon Street, Port Melbourne, Victoria 3207

Designed by Louise Lavarack
Photographs by Rodney Weidland
Styling by Margaret Alcock
Food cooked by Jill Pavey, Nina Harris, Tim MacFarlane Reid
China: Noritake (Australia) Pty Ltd; Waterford Wedgwood Australia Ltd;
Villeroy & Boch (Aust) Pty Ltd; Royal Doulton Australia Pty Ltd
Ceramic bowls from Made in Japan, Neutral Bay, NSW
Typeset in 9½/12pt Berkeley Old Style Book by Midland Typesetters
Produced in Hong Kong by Mandarin Offset

National Library of Australia
    cataloguing-in-publication data:

Solomon, Charmaine.
    Oriental banquets.

    Includes index.
    ISBN 0 947334 46 7.

    1. Cookery, Oriental. 2. Dinners and dining. I. Title. (Series:
    Solomon, Charmaine. Charmaine Solomon's Asian cooking library).

641.595

Introduction

This little book will help you to entertain in exotic oriental style, impress your guests, delight the gourmet palate, and all without having to call in caterers.

Nothing happens without some effort, but there is no need to wear yourself out. With clever planning and reliable, authentic recipes, you can create the great dishes of India, Malaysia, Indonesia, Thailand, China and other fascinating places.

What's more, when entertaining Asian style all the dishes are brought to the table at once—there is no need for different courses on different plates. Host and hostess can sit down with the guests, relax and enjoy.

Rice In Asia, when they want to know if you have dined the question asked is, 'Have you eaten rice?' Rice is the main event in an Asian meal so it is of vital importance to be able to cook this grain perfectly.

With a modicum of care taken in measuring rice and liquid and a reliable kitchen timer for timing the cooking, there is no problem in getting the desired result every time. The aim is to keep a steady low heat, preventing scorching of the base of the pan and the bottom layer of rice. Because I prefer to use stainless steel pans and they are not always as heavy as I would like, I put a flame tamer or heat diffuser under the pan. If you are able to turn the heat down really low, however, there is no problem.

Of course, you could invest in the wonderful electric rice cooker. Apart from cooking plain steamed rice perfectly, it is possible to make pilaus and birianis if the frying of the spice, onions and rice is done in another pan and then transferred to the rice cooker with stock or other liquid. (It is important to remember, however, that while hot stock is added when cooking in a saucepan, stock should be at room temperature if using the electric rice cooker.) I never thought I needed a rice cooker, but have to admit that using one has meant extra liberation. Not only is the rice cooked perfectly, it is kept warm until needed. I am totally converted.

Drinks With Far Eastern meals the perfect accompaniment is pale, fragrant Chinese tea—not only does it complement the food, it also settles the digestion when you are carried away by delicious flavours and eat perhaps more than you ought. Chinese tea is never served with sugar or milk, and is made with only one teaspoon of tea to a pot which holds 4 standard measuring cups of water. More boiling water can be added as the tea stands and becomes stronger. After a couple of additions, rinse out the pot and start again.

With South-East Asian food, sweet drinks such as fruit juices are ideal. If you must have wine, a light, fruity white is the answer—gewurztraminer, Riesling or a somewhat drier white. But certainly not a big red wine with lots of tannin—you would enjoy neither the wine nor the food.

Indian meals seem to taste even better when accompanied by ice-cold lassi (yoghurt or buttermilk whisked with water or soda), lightly sweetened or salted. Sometimes a few drops of rose water or a pinch of cardamom may be added, but any flavour must be added very sparingly. Just as suitable is nimboo pani—fresh lime juice mixed with iced water (or soda) and sweetened to taste with sugar. But it is also a fact that ice-cold lager or beer shandy is much favoured with curry meals.

North India

The food of North India is rich (note the use of ghee as a cooking medium), uses fragrant spices and is not hot—only a passing nod is given to chillies. The flavours here are mainly Moghul style, reflecting the grandeur of the emperors of old. The fragrance of saffron, cardamom and rose water haunts not only the sweets, but also the main dishes.

A menu like this one is ideal for a large party: there are a number of dishes and something is bound to appeal to everybody.

Serves 12

A classic dish called Doh Piaza—*a richly spiced curry which is not too hot.*

Lamb Curry

- 2 kg (4 lb) boned lamb (from shoulder or leg)
- 1 kg (2 lb) onions
- 8 large cloves garlic, peeled
- ½ cup chopped coriander leaves
- 1 tablespoon chopped fresh ginger
- ½ cup plain yoghurt
- 2 teaspoons chilli powder, or to taste
- 1 teaspoon paprika
- 3 tablespoons ground coriander
- 1 tablespoon kalonji (nigella) seeds
- 3 tablespoons ghee
- 3 tablespoons oil
- 10 cardamom pods, bruised
- 2 teaspoons garam masala
- 3 teaspoons salt or to taste

Trim off fat and cut meat into large cubes. Finely slice half the onions. Roughly chop remaining onions and put into food processor or blender with garlic, coriander leaves, ginger, yoghurt, chilli powder, paprika, ground coriander and kalonji seeds. Process until smooth.

Heat ghee and oil in a large heavy pan and fry sliced onions, stirring frequently, until evenly browned. Remove from pan. Add cubed lamb to pan, a little at a time, and stir-fry over high heat until browned all over. Remove each batch as it browns before adding more. When all meat is browned, lower heat to medium. Add a little more oil to pan if necessary and fry blended mixture, stirring, until it is aromatic. This takes quite a while—20 minutes or longer—and when it is ready oil will appear around edges of mixture.

Return meat to pan, add cardamom pods and salt, stir until well mixed. Cover and cook over low heat until meat is almost tender, stirring occasionally. The juices given out by the meat are usually sufficient to finish the cooking, but it may be necessary to add a little water. When meat is tender and liquid almost absorbed, add garam masala and reserved fried onion slices. Cover pan and simmer gently a few minutes longer.

Such a simple recipe but so much flavour. Just be sure the saffron you use is the genuine article—there are many worthless imitations, usually marigold or safflower, which are similar in colour but have none of the fragrance or flavour. I find it best to buy from a chefs' supplier even though the minimum quantity is fairly large. Saffron keeps well in the freezer.

SAFFRON CHICKEN

- 2 kg (4 lb) chicken pieces (thighs, wings, drumsticks and half-breasts)
- 4 tablespoons ghee
- 2 large onions, chopped finely
- 6 cloves garlic, chopped finely
- 1 tablespoon finely grated fresh ginger
- 5 fresh red chillies, seeded and sliced
- ½ teaspoon saffron threads
- 1 teaspoon ground cardamom
- 1½ teaspoons salt or to taste

Wash and dry chicken pieces well. Cut half-breasts into halves again. Heat ghee in a large heavy saucepan or flameproof casserole and fry onion, garlic, ginger and chillies over gentle heat, stirring frequently, until onion is soft and beginning to turn golden. Meanwhile, lightly toast saffron threads in a small heavy pan—don't let them burn—turn into a bowl, crush to powder with the back of a spoon and dissolve in 2 tablespoons boiling water. Add to saucepan with cardamom and stir well. Add chicken in batches, increase heat and toss in saffron mixture for about 5 minutes or until each piece is golden. Stir in salt, cover and cook over moderate heat until chicken is almost tender. Uncover pan and cook until liquid has reduced.

Savoury Potatoes and Peas

- 4 tablespoons ghee or oil
- 4 medium onions, chopped finely
- 2 teaspoons finely grated fresh ginger
- 2 teaspoons black mustard seeds
- 1 teaspoon kalonji (nigella) seeds
- 1 teaspoon ground turmeric
- 1 teaspoon chilli powder
- 1 teaspoon salt or to taste
- 1 kg (2 lb) potatoes, peeled and diced
- 2 cups frozen peas, thawed

Heat ghee or oil in a large heavy saucepan and fry onions with ginger, mustard and kalonji seeds. Cook until onions are soft and golden. Stir in turmeric, chilli powder and salt. Toss potatoes in this mixture for 5 minutes. Add ¾ cup hot water, cover tightly and cook over very low heat for 20 minutes. Stir in peas, replace lid and cook for a further 10 minutes.

Note   In Indian grocery stores you can buy good quality sweet chutneys and hot pickles to serve as extra accompaniments to the banquet. Here, too, you will find the spicy lentil wafers known as pappadams which are quickly deep fried in hot oil, drained on absorbent paper and served as a crisp addition to the meal.

SPICY PILAU RICE

- 1.5 kg (3 lb) chicken soup pieces or 4 lamb shanks
- 6 cardamom pods, bruised
- 1 teaspoon black peppercorns
- 1 tablespoon salt
- 1 large onion stuck with 5 cloves
- 1 kg (2 lb) basmati rice
- 4 tablespoons ghee
- 1 large onion, finely sliced
- ½ teaspoon saffron threads
- 2 teaspoons finely grated fresh ginger
- 1 teaspoon garam masala
- 1 teaspoon ground cardamom
- 2 tablespoons rose water (see Note)
- ½ cup sultanas
- ¾ cup fried blanched almonds
- 4 hard-boiled eggs, quartered

To make a strong, well-flavoured stock, place chicken pieces or lamb shanks in a large pot with cardamom pods, peppercorns, salt and onion stuck with cloves. Cover with plenty of water (about 3 L) and bring to boil. Reduce heat and simmer, covered, for about 2 hours. Cool slightly, strain and measure out 8 cups (the remainder may be used in other recipes or frozen). Taste stock and, if necessary, add extra salt to taste. (Alternatively, make up 8 cups using instant chicken stock, add aromatic ingredients—minus the salt—and simmer for 30 minutes.)

Meanwhile wash rice thoroughly in water, drain in a large colander and allow to dry for at least 30 minutes. Heat ghee in a large saucepan and fry sliced onion until golden. Toast saffron threads lightly in a small dry pan—watch that they don't burn—transfer to a dish, crush with the back of a spoon and dissolve in 1 tablespoon hot water. Add saffron and ginger to saucepan and fry for 1 minute, stirring constantly. Add rice, and fry a few minutes longer over a moderate heat. Stir carefully with a slotted metal spoon to prevent breaking up the delicate rice grains. Add the 8 cups of hot stock, garam masala, cardamom, rose water and sultanas. Stir well. Bring quickly to boil, cover pan with a tightly fitting lid and cook over a very low heat for 20 minutes. Do not uncover saucepan or stir rice during cooking time.

When rice is cooked, remove from heat and leave uncovered for 5 minutes so steam can escape. Fluff gently with a fork and transfer to a serving dish with a slotted metal spoon. Garnish with almonds and quartered eggs.

Note   Be careful not to confuse rose water with rose essence. Rose water is available from chemists or Asian food stores and is very lightly perfumed. Rose essence, usually sold along with other flavouring essences, is highly concentrated and only a few drops should be used, say ¼ teaspoon.

A cooling accompaniment to any curry meal.

YOGHURT WITH CUCUMBERS

- *1 large, thin-skinned cucumber or 4 small seedless cucumbers*
- *salt*
- *¼ cup finely chopped mint*
- *1½ cups thick sour cream*
- *1½ cups plain yoghurt*
- *lemon juice to taste*
- *3 teaspoons cummin seeds*
- *mint sprigs*

Wash cucumbers but do not peel unless you are only able to get the thick-skinned variety. Cut in halves lengthways and if seeds are well developed, scoop them out and discard. Cut cucumbers into small dice. Sprinkle with salt and place in a colander for 15 minutes to allow liquid to drain away. Rinse quickly with cold water. Leave to drain well.

Combine cucumbers in a bowl with mint, sour cream, yoghurt and lemon juice. Taste to see if more salt is required.

Toast cummin seeds in a dry pan for a few minutes, stirring constantly until fragrant and a darker brown. Crush seeds and sprinkle over yoghurt mixture. Serve chilled, garnished with mint sprigs.

In India grinding stones are used for making fresh chutneys and 'wet' masalas. A mortar and pestle is a good substitute, but for today's cook a blender or food processor is ideal.

Coriander Chutney

- 12 spring onions, including green tops, chopped
- 2 cups firmly packed coriander leaves
- 3 fresh green chillies, roughly chopped
- 1 large clove garlic, chopped
- 2 teaspoons salt
- 1 tablespoon sugar
- 2 teaspoons garam masala
- ½ cup lemon juice

Place all ingredients in blender or food processor and blend to a smooth purée with ¼ cup water, scraping sides of container as necessary.

If using a mortar and pestle, finely chop spring onions, coriander, chillies and garlic. Pound a little at a time until a paste forms, then mix in remaining ingredients.

Pour the chutney into a small bowl, cover and chill. May be stored up to 2 days.

A sweet drink especially popular at grand banquets.

FALOODA

- *1 tablespoon tulsi (basil) seeds*
- *rose-flavoured syrup (see Note)*
- *agar-agar jelly (see below)*
- *ice-cold milk*
- *crushed ice*

Soak the tulsi seeds in cold water for 10 minutes.

In each glass put 1 or 2 tablespoons of rose-flavoured syrup, fill with cold milk and add some crushed ice. Stir well. Add a teaspoonful of soaked tulsi seeds to each glass and some finely diced jelly if desired.

JELLY
- *2 teaspoons agar-agar powder*
- *½ cup white sugar*
- *red and green food colouring*
- *rose flavouring*

Sprinkle agar-agar over 2 cups water in a saucepan, add sugar and boil, stirring until agar-agar is completely dissolved. Divide in two, add red food colouring and a drop of rose essence to one portion. Colour other portion green. Pour into large shallow dishes and leave to set. Cut into tiny dice.

Note If unable to purchase rose syrup at an Indian store, make it at home by dissolving 3 cups white sugar in 2 cups water over low heat. Cool, flavour with 1 teaspoon rose essence and colour a strong red or pink with food colouring. Dilute with milk or iced water.

Can be made a day or two ahead.

Carrot Halva

- *60 g (2 oz) ghee*
- *5 cardamom pods, bruised*
- *750 g (1½ lb) carrots, peeled and grated*
- *2 cups sugar*
- *½ cup full cream milk powder*
- *¾ cup evaporated milk*
- *2 teaspoons rose water (see Note on p. 6)*
- *2 tablespoons blanched pistachios*
- *edible silver or gold leaf, optional*

Heat ghee in a heavy saucepan and add cardamom pods and grated carrots. Stir well, cover and cook over low heat for 10 minutes, then uncover and stir until any liquid has evaporated.

Meanwhile, make a syrup with sugar and ¾ cup water, boiling it hard for 5 minutes. Mix milk powder and evaporated milk until smooth and add, with sugar syrup, to carrots. Cook, stirring constantly, until mixture forms a mass and comes away from side of pan. Remove from heat and add rose water. Pour into a greased dish, sprinkle with roughly chopped pistachios and gently press onto surface. When cold, cut into squares. You can decorate top with edible silver or gold leaf—the latter is a pricey little item but very much part of the show when entertaining guests in the style of the Maharajahs!

Note When all ingredients are combined halva may be cooked in a very large microwave proof bowl, in microwave on full power, stirring every 5 minutes until very thick.

Sri Lanka

Sri Lanka's special occasion food borrows from cuisines of nations which have, over the centuries, been rulers and traders in this island. Its favourite flavours are those bequeathed by the Dutch and the Malays.

Serves 12

Pronounce the word 'lampries' something like 'lump rice' but with a 'z' sound at the end of 'rice', and you won't be far wrong. The name is derived from the Dutch word, lomprijst, *a combination of rice cooked in stock, Dutch-style forcemeat balls, Sinhalese curries and sambols. Just as an elaborate pilau is the ultimate in festive meals in India, lampries mark a 'special occasion' in Sri Lanka.*

LAMPRIES

The various components of lampries are put together in individual servings, each one containing a cupful of cooked rice, a couple of tablespoons of curry, 2 meatballs and so on, wrapped in banana leaves and baked, which gives the whole thing a subtle but lovely extra aroma and flavour. Select large, wide banana leaves, strip them from the centre rib and cut into pieces approximately 30 to 38 cm (12 to 15 in) long. Wash, dry with a clean cloth and heat over a gas flame for a few seconds on each side. This makes them pliable and they will fold without splitting. Alternatively, put banana leaves in a large basin or sink and pour boiling water over. If no banana leaves are available, substitute 38 cm (15 in) squares of aluminium foil.

It's best to have someone help you prepare this banquet, but if you must do it alone, make all the dishes (except the

rice) 2 days ahead and refrigerate—this will improve the flavour as well. When making the parcels, set up your work space like an assembly line. This may seem like a great deal of work, but as it is all done in advance there's virtually nothing more to do once the lampries are served.

On each piece of leaf or foil place 1 cup firmly packed Ghee Rice. Around the rice arrange 2 tablespoons Four Meat Curry, 2 Dutch-style Meatballs, 2 teaspoons Eggplant Pickle, 1 heaped teaspoon Chilli Sambol and 1 heaped teaspoon Prawn Blachan. Pour a tablespoon of coconut milk over the rice. You can use canned coconut milk, diluted with an equal amount of water.

If using a leaf, fold over and fasten with bamboo skewers. You can also enclose leaf parcels in aluminium foil; this is a good protection in case the leaf splits while heating or serving. Fold foil over to make a neat oblong package. Heat lampries in a moderate oven for approximately 20 to 25 minutes. Arrange on a large serving dish or tray. The Cucumber Sambol is not included in the parcel, but is served alongside as a cool accompaniment.

When your guests open the lampries they will be amazed at the wonderful fragrance which comes from this appetizing dish. It is usual to allow 2 lampries each for hearty eaters.

Note   It is a good idea to make a large number of lampries as they are ideal for parties and wonderful for picnics. They freeze well and may be kept frozen for 3 months. Heat in a moderate oven 170° to 190° C (350° to 375° F) from frozen state for 40 minutes or 25 minutes if first thawed to room temperature.

11

Four Meat Curry

- 500 g (1 lb) boneless blade steak
- 500 g (1 lb) lean boneless lamb
- 8 cardamom pods
- 20 black peppercorns
- 5 teaspoons salt
- 750 g (1½ lb) chicken thighs
- 750 g (1½ lb) pork shoulder or loin
- 2 tablespoons ghee
- 2 tablespoons peanut oil
- 2 cups finely chopped onions
- 2 tablespoons finely chopped garlic
- 1 tablespoon finely chopped fresh ginger
- sprig of fresh or 12 dried curry leaves
- ¼ teaspoon fenugreek seeds, optional
- 4 tablespoons Ceylon curry powder
- 1 teaspoon ground turmeric
- 2 teaspoons chilli powder
- 1 cinnamon stick
- 2 teaspoons ground cardamom
- 1 fresh or 6 to 8 strips dried pandan leaf
- 2 stalks lemon grass, bruised and tied in a knot or 4 strips lemon rind
- juice of 1 lemon
- 3 cups thin coconut milk (see Note)
- 2 cups thick coconut milk (see Note)

Put steak and lamb in a large saucepan. Cover with cold water; add cardamom pods, peppercorns and half the salt. Cover pan, bring to boil and simmer for 30 minutes. Add chicken and simmer for a further 15 minutes. Allow to cool slightly. Strain and reserve stock for cooking rice. Cut parboiled meats into very small dice. Dice the pork.

Heat ghee and oil in a large saucepan and gently fry onion, garlic, ginger and curry leaves until onion is soft and starts to turn golden. Add fenugreek seeds if used and fry for 1 minute. Add curry powder, turmeric, chilli powder, cinnamon stick, cardamom, pandan leaf, and lemon grass or lemon rind. Add remaining 2 teaspoons salt, lemon juice, diced pork and thin coconut milk. Stir well. Cover and cook over a low heat for 30 minutes.

Add parboiled meats and thick coconut milk and simmer uncovered for about 1½ hours, or until meat is tender and gravy reduced. Remove cinnamon stick, pandan leaf and lemon grass before serving.

Note For thick coconut milk dilute canned coconut milk with an equal amount of water; for thin coconut milk dilute with 2 parts water to 1 part coconut milk.

Remembering that the Dutch East India Company brought many settlers to the area, it isn't surprising that many dishes now accepted as Sri Lankan had their beginnings in a land far away, then gathered spicy momentum from their land of adoption.

DUTCH-STYLE MEATBALLS
Makes about 40

- *30 g (1 oz) butter*
- *1 cup finely chopped onion*
- *500 g (1 lb) minced steak*
- *½ cup soft white breadcrumbs*
- *1½ teaspoons salt*
- *½ teaspoon ground black pepper*

- 2 teaspoons chopped fresh dill
- ¼ teaspoon ground cinnamon
- ¼ teaspoon ground cloves
- 1 teaspoon crushed garlic
- ½ teaspoon finely grated fresh ginger
- squeeze of lemon juice
- 1 egg, beaten
- dry breadcrumbs for coating
- oil for frying

Heat butter in a small frying pan and gently fry onion until soft. Combine with minced steak, breadcrumbs, salt, pepper, chopped dill, cinnamon, cloves, garlic, ginger and lemon juice. Mix thoroughly and form into small balls (about 3 cm (1¼ in) in diameter). Dip into beaten egg and coat with dry breadcrumbs. Deep-fry in hot oil until golden brown. Drain on paper towels before serving.

Eggplant Pickle

- 1 kg (2 lb) eggplant
- 2 teaspoons salt
- 2 teaspoons ground turmeric
- oil for frying
- 1 tablespoon black mustard seeds
- ½ cup malt vinegar
- 1 medium onion, finely chopped
- 4 cloves garlic, sliced
- 1 tablespoon finely chopped fresh ginger
- 2 tablespoons Ceylon curry powder
- ½ cup dried tamarind
- 3 fresh green chillies, seeded and sliced
- small cinnamon stick
- 1 teaspoon chilli powder
- 1 tablespoon sugar
- extra salt to taste

Cut eggplant into thin slices, rub with salt and turmeric and place in colander. Stand for 1 hour at least, allowing to drain. Dry eggplant on paper towels. Heat about 2.5 cm (1 in) oil in a large frying pan and fry slices of eggplant quite slowly until brown on both sides. Remove with a slotted spoon or spatula and place in a bowl. Reserve remaining oil used in frying.

Place mustard seeds and vinegar in blender, cover and blend on high speed until mustard is ground. Add onion, garlic and ginger and blend until a smooth paste is formed. Set aside.

Soak tamarind pulp in ¾ cup hot water, squeeze then strain and discard seeds, reserving liquid.

Heat ½ cup of reserved oil and fry mustard mixture for 5 minutes. Add curry powder, chillies, cinnamon stick, chilli powder and tamarind liquid. Stir and add fried eggplant slices and any oil that has collected in the bowl. Cover and simmer for 15 minutes. Remove from heat and stir in sugar. Add extra salt to taste.

Allow to cool completely and transfer to clean, dry jars for storage. Keeps in refrigerator for up to 2 months.

Note A food processor will not grind mustard seeds successfully. In the absence of a blender, crush seeds in a mortar and pestle. Use the pestle with a rotating motion so that the seeds do not jump out of the mortar.

CHILLI SAMBOL

- ½ cup peanut oil
- 4 medium onions, finely sliced
- 3 teaspoons chilli powder
- 125 g (4 oz) dried prawn powder
- 3 tablespoons malt vinegar
- 1 cup canned coconut milk
- salt to taste
- 1 tablespoon brown sugar

Heat oil in a large frying pan and fry onion very slowly, stirring from time to time, until soft and transparent. (It is important to fry onions slowly, not only to prevent them burning but to evaporate all liquid so that sambol will keep well.) When onion is golden, add chilli powder, prawns, vinegar and coconut milk. Stir thoroughly and simmer, covered, for 10 minutes. Remove cover and continue simmering, stirring occasionally, until liquid evaporates and oil starts to separate from mixture. Season to taste with salt. Remove from heat and stir in sugar. Leave to cool before transferring to a clean, dry jar. Store in refrigerator up to 6 weeks. Use in small quantities.

Note   Dried prawn powder is sold in packets in Asian stores.

Prawn Blachan

- 1 cup dried prawn powder
- ½ cup desiccated coconut
- 2 teaspoons chilli powder or to taste
- 2 medium onions, chopped
- 3 teaspoons crushed garlic
- 1 tablespoon finely chopped fresh ginger

⅔ cup lemon juice

- 1 teaspoon salt, or to taste

Heat prawn powder in a dry frying pan, stirring continuously for a few minutes. Turn out onto a large plate. Place coconut in the same frying pan and toast, stirring constantly, until it turns a deep brown colour. Transfer to a plate to cool.

Purée remaining ingredients in a blender or food processor, add prawn powder and coconut and blend again, scraping down sides of container with a spatula from time to time. If absolutely necessary add a little water to facilitate blending. It should be thick enough to mound.

Ghee Rice

- 1.5 kg (3 lb) basmati rice
- 90 g (3 oz) ghee
- 3 tablespoons oil
- 3 large onions, finely sliced
- 10 whole cloves
- 10 cardamom pods, bruised
- 3 small sticks cinnamon
- 10 cups hot stock (see Four Meat Curry, page 12)
- 1 tablespoon salt

Wash rice well and drain for at least 30 minutes. Heat ghee and oil in a large saucepan and fry onion until golden; add spices and drained rice. Fry, stirring with a slotted metal spoon, for 5 minutes over moderate heat. Add hot stock and salt and bring to boil.

Reduce heat to very low. Cover pan tightly and cook for 15 to 20 minutes—do not lift lid during this time. At end of cooking time, uncover and allow steam to escape for 5 minutes. Gently fluff up rice with fork and remove whole spices. Leave to cool.

CUCUMBER SAMBOL

- *2 large or 6 small seedless cucumbers*
- *salt*
- *1 cup thick coconut milk (see Note)*
- *3 fresh red chillies, seeded and sliced*
- *3 fresh green chillies, seeded and sliced*
- *1 large onion, cut into paper-thin slices*
- *lemon juice to taste*

Wash and peel cucumbers, halve lengthways (and remove seeds if not able to buy seedless variety). Slice very thinly. Place in colander, sprinkling layers with salt and allow to stand and drain for at least 30 minutes. Press out all liquid and if too salty rinse with cold water. Drain well. Mix with remaining ingredients. Cover and chill until ready to serve.

Note In this recipe use canned coconut milk undiluted. Canned coconut milk varies in thickness from one brand to another. If the brand you purchase is so thick it is almost solid, heat it slightly to pouring consistency. If still too thick, add a little water. It should be about as thick as pouring cream.

Serve as a dessert after lampries.

SPICY COCONUT CUSTARD

- *250 g (8 oz) dark palm sugar (jaggery)*
- *6 eggs*
- *1 cup canned coconut milk*
- *1 x 375 mL can evaporated milk*
- *1 teaspoon ground cardamom*
- *1 teaspoon freshly grated nutmeg*
- *¼ teaspoon ground cloves*
- *2 tablespoons rose water (see Note, p. 6)*

Chop palm sugar into small pieces. Heat ¾ cup water with palm sugar in a saucepan and dissolve over low heat; allow to cool. Add palm sugar syrup to slightly beaten eggs, stir in coconut milk and ½ cup water. Strain through a fine strainer into a large jug. Stir in evaporated milk, spices and rose water. Pour into individual custard cups placed in a baking dish. Pour water into baking dish to come halfway up sides of cups and cook in a slow oven until set—about 40 minutes. Allow custards to cool and chill before serving.

Note You can, decorate tops of custards with raw cashew halves.

SINGAPORE

A typical Nonya menu reflecting the blend of Malay and Chinese influences which make the cooking of Singapore so individual.

Serves 6 to 8

This recipe seems to have a lot of steps just to cook rice, but the end result—the grains firm and separate, yet rich with coconut milk—justifies the process.

STEAMED COCONUT RICE

- *3 cups long grain rice*
- *1 cup canned coconut milk*
- *2 teaspoons salt or to taste*

Soak rice in cold water overnight. Drain and spread in the top part of a steamer and steam over rapidly boiling water for 30 minutes. Halfway through steaming, stir so that rice on the bottom is brought to the top. Gently heat coconut milk, ½ cup water and salt in a large saucepan, stirring. Do not let it boil. Turn off heat, add steamed rice and stir well. Cover tightly and let stand for a further 30 minutes. At the end of this time the milk should be completely absorbed. Spread rice once more in top of steamer, bring water back to boil and steam for 30 minutes. Progressively lower heat until water is just simmering. Serve hot.

A dish usually made during the Chinese New Year since everyone is on holidays (even the cooks!); the acid preserves the meat over the holiday period.

CHICKEN IN TAMARIND

- *1 x 1.6 kg roasting chicken, preferably free-range*
- *¾ cup dried tamarind*
- *20 golden shallots or 3 brown onions*
- *3 tablespoons ground coriander*
- *3 tablespoons malt vinegar*
- *2 tablespoons dark soy sauce*
- *6 tablespoons sugar*
- *3 teaspoons instant chicken stock*
- *2 teaspoons ground black pepper*
- *1 teaspoon salt*
- *peanut oil for frying*

Cut chicken in halves lengthwise and put into a large glass or earthenware bowl. Pour 2 cups warm water over tamarind and leave to soften for 5 minutes, then squeeze firmly to dissolve all pulp. Strain through a sieve and reserve pulp, discarding seeds and fibres. Peel shallots or onions, chop roughly and grind to a purée in food processor or blender. Combine with tamarind pulp and all other ingredients except oil. Pour over and around chicken, place a weighted plate on top to keep chicken immersed in marinade and leave overnight or at least

8 hours. (Because of acid content in marinade it is not advisable to use aluminium utensils.) Transfer chicken to a stainless steel or enamel saucepan, bring to boil and simmer until tender. Remove from heat and allow to cool, then take out chicken and cut into serving pieces.

Heat a wok or heavy frying pan and add enough peanut oil to cover base. When oil is hot, fry chicken, a few pieces at a time, until browned on all sides. Remove from pan as each batch is fried. Pour off oil, add tamarind marinade to pan and cook over high heat until reduced and thick, stirring frequently. Pour over chicken and serve with steamed coconut rice and sambals.

PRAWN AND CHILLI SAMBAL

- *500 g (1 lb) small raw prawns*
- *2 teaspoons crushed garlic*
- *3 teaspoons sambal olek or finely chopped hot chillies*
- *2 teaspoons finely grated fresh ginger*
- *oil for frying*
- *1 tablespoon sugar*
- *1 tablespoon light soy sauce*
- *1 tablespoon dry sherry*

Shell and devein prawns, rinse and dry well on paper towel. Crush garlic with a little of the sugar and mix with sambal oelek and ginger. Heat ½ cup oil in wok until very hot. Deep fry prawns in small batches just until the colour changes— do not overcook. Remove from pan and drain on paper towel. Pour off oil from pan, leaving 1 tablespoon. Add garlic mixture and fry over low heat, stirring. Add remaining sugar, soy sauce and dry sherry, then add prawns and stir only until reheated. Serve immediately.

Pork and Cucumber Sambal

- *2 pork loin chops*
- *⅓ cup dried prawns*
- *3 tablespoons peanut oil*
- *1 teaspoon crushed garlic*
- *3 or 4 fresh red chillies, sliced*
- *1 tablespoon fish sauce*
- *3 teaspoons sugar*
- *2 tablespoons lime or lemon juice*
- *4 small seedless cucumbers*
- *¾ cup toasted, salted peanuts*
- *3 tablespoons chopped laksa leaf or spring onions*

Cut off and discard skin and slice chops into thin strips. Soak prawns in warm water for 10 minutes. Drain and crush in mortar and pestle or in food processor.

Heat oil in a wok and fry pork strips until brown. Add garlic, prawns and chillies and stir-fry for a few minutes longer. Add fish sauce, sugar and lime juice; stir until sugar dissolves and liquid reduces. Remove to a bowl and allow to cool.

Wash cucumbers but do not peel unless skin is very tough. Shortly before serving, cut into thick slices or small wedges and toss with fried mixture until well mixed. Crush peanuts in a food processor or with mortar and pestle and, with chopped fresh herbs, sprinkle over fried mixture.

PINEAPPLE TARTS
Makes about 24

- 1 x 850 g can crushed pineapple pieces
  - 1½ cups sugar
  - 1 stick cinnamon
  - 2 tablespoons semolina
  - 2 tablespoons pineapple juice
  - 2 cups plain flour
  - 125g unsalted butter
  - ½ cup caster sugar
  - 1 egg yolk
- 1 teaspoon vanilla essence
  - extra egg yolk

Drain pineapple well, pressing out and reserving syrup. Put drained pineapple into a heavy pan, add sugar and cinnamon. Bring to boil and stir over medium heat for 15 minutes.

Mix semolina with 2 tablespoons pineapple syrup, stirring out any lumps. Add to pan and stir constantly for 15 minutes until mixture is thick. Allow to cool completely.

Sift flour into a bowl. Cut butter into small pieces and rub in lightly with fingertips. Add caster sugar and mix. Beat egg yolk and vanilla, adding 2 tablespoons iced water. Pour over flour and mix gently, adding an extra tablespoon of water if necessary to make a soft dough. Wrap in plastic and chill for 30 minutes.

Take half the pastry and, on a lightly floured surface, roll out to a rectangle about 3 mm thick. Cut into smaller rectangles 6 cm x 9 cm. Put a teaspoon of pineapple filling in the centre of each one and fold over the 2 short ends so that there is a double layer of pastry on the top. Trim corners, pinch ends together to make a pineapple shape and seal jam in. Brush with beaten egg yolk to glaze, then with scissors make little snips in top layer of pastry.

Transfer to a baking sheet lined with baking parchment or foil. Bake in preheated moderately hot oven 15 minutes or until pastry is golden. If preferred, make small tartlets.

In Singapore ask for Ice Kacang and you are served a cone of shaved ice piled high over sweet beans, palm sugar seeds and Chinese dried fruits, and drizzled with coloured syrup.

SNOW CONE WITH SWEET SURPRISES

- *1 cup palm sugar seeds in syrup*
- *½ cup sweet red beans in syrup*
- *1 cup small preserved plums or canned jakfruit in syrup, chopped*
- *1 cup canned grass jelly, sliced or agar-agar jelly (see p. 8)*
- *block ice or ice cubes*
- *1 cup rose-flavoured syrup, or to taste*

Put a few palm sugar seeds, sweet beans, 3 or 4 preserved plums or spoonful of jakfruit, and some grass jelly in each dessert dish. These can be assembled ahead of time.

Just before serving, shave ice block (machines to do this are sold at some Asian shops) or put ice cubes into food processor with steel blades and process in bursts until ice turns to fine snow. Pile on each plate, drizzle syrup over and serve at once. Top with a scoop of ice cream if liked.

Note Grass jelly is translucent, brownish black and tastes strongly of the sea. Agar-agar jelly may be substituted.

MALAYSIA

To extend this banquet choose dishes from Indonesia, Sri Lanka and Singapore—the flavours will blend perfectly. Avoid pork which is taboo to Moslems and Malaysia is predominantly Moslem. Serve with Steamed Rice (see p. 44) or Ghee Rice (see p. 17).

Serves 6 to 8

CHICKEN AND COCONUT CURRY

- ½ cup desiccated coconut
- 2 to 3 teaspoons sambal oelek or 3 fresh red chillies
- 2 medium onions
- 2 teaspoons chopped garlic
- 1 tablespoon chopped galangal (see Note)
- 5 teaspoons ground coriander
- 3 teaspoons ground cummin
- 1 teaspoon ground turmeric
- 1 teaspoon dried shrimp paste
- 1 stalk lemon grass, sliced thinly or 3 strips lemon rind
- 2 tablespoons peanut oil
- 1 cup canned coconut milk, diluted (see Note)
- 1½ teaspoons salt, or to taste
- 6 chicken drumsticks
- 6 chicken thighs

In a dry pan toast coconut, stirring or shaking pan so coconut colours evenly. Toast until it is a very deep brown, almost coffee-brown. (It is the dark roasting which gives the distinctive flavour to this particular curry.) Turn onto a plate to prevent burning (it most certainly will if left in the hot pan). When cool, put coconut into an electric blender (a food processor

won't grind it finely enough) or use a mortar and pestle to pound it finely. If using a blender, add ½ cup water or sufficient to work it to a smooth purée. Transfer coconut to a bowl.

Without washing out the blender, process chillies, onions, garlic, galangal, coriander, ground spices, shrimp paste and lemon grass to a smooth purée, adding a little of the coconut milk if necessary to facilitate blending.

Heat oil in a heavy saucepan and fry blended mixture on low heat, stirring frequently, for about 15 minutes or until it smells fragrant and oil shines on the surface. Add toasted and ground coconut, coconut milk and salt. Add chicken and stir until mixture comes to boil. Turn heat down to simmer and cook, uncovered, until chicken is tender and cooked through.

This curry improves when it is made a day or two ahead and kept covered in the refrigerator. Reheat gently.

Note Canned coconut milk is the easiest to use, and for this recipe it should be diluted with an equal amount of water. Any unused coconut milk should be poured into ice cube trays and frozen, then stored in a freezer bag until needed.

Galangal may be fresh, frozen or pickled in brine. If only available dried and ground, reduce quantity to 2 teaspoons.

Squid Sambal

- 500 g (1 lb) cleaned squid
- 2 onions, chopped roughly
- 2 cloves garlic
- 1 teaspoon dried shrimp paste
- 1 stalk fresh lemon grass, finely sliced or 2 strips lemon rind
- 6 fresh red chillies
- 1 tablespoon dried tamarind
- 3 tablespoons peanut oil
- 2 teaspoons brown sugar

Wash squid well, paying particular attention to inside where sand may lurk; pat dry with paper towel and cut across into rings. Set aside. Put onion, garlic, shrimp paste, lemon grass or rind and chillies in food processor or blender and process until smooth, adding a little water if necessary to facilitate blending.

Soak tamarind pulp in ½ cup hot water for 5 minutes or until soft. Squeeze to dissolve pulp then strain out seeds and fibre, reserving liquid. Heat oil in a wok or frying pan and add chilli mixture. Cook, stirring, over medium heat until it becomes dark in colour and a film of oil shines on surface. Add tamarind liquid, sugar and, when boiling, squid. Cook uncovered, stirring, until squid is cooked and mixture is thick and oily.

CURRIED CUCUMBERS

- *1 large or 4 small seedless cucumbers*
- *1 small onion, chopped*
- *2 fresh green chillies*
- *1 teaspoon finely grated fresh ginger*
- *2 cloves garlic, chopped*
- *¼ teaspoon ground turmeric*
- *2 cups canned coconut milk*
- *salt to taste*
- *1 tablespoon lemon juice*

Wash cucumber, cut in halves, then quarters lengthwise and across into small chunks. (If seedless cucumbers are not available use 2 of the more common variety, peel and remove seeds.) Place onion, chillies, ginger, garlic, turmeric, 1½ cups of the canned coconut milk, 1½ cups water and salt to taste in a saucepan. Simmer gently until onion is tender. Add cucumber and remaining ½ cup of coconut milk. Cook, uncovered, for 10 minutes, stirring occasionally. Remove from heat and stir in lemon juice. Add extra salt to taste if necessary.

The sweetness of dates and sultanas, the sharpness of vinegar and spices, the crunch of partly cooked vegetables, all contribute to the popularity of this relish.

FRUIT AND VEGETABLE PICKLE

- *1 cup dates, chopped*
- *1 cup sultanas*
- *2 cups vinegar*
- *¾ cup sugar*
- *1 cup small cauliflower sprigs*
- *1 cup julienne-cut carrots*
- *1 cup sliced green beans*
- *1 cup peeled golden shallots*
- *2 tablespoons peanut oil*

- *2 teaspoons crushed garlic*
- *2 teaspoons finely grated ginger*
- *1 tablespoon ground black mustard*
- *1 tablespoon chilli paste or powder*
- *2 teaspoons ground fennel*

Soak dates and sultanas in vinegar and 1 cup water for an hour, then add sugar and boil until soft. Add vegetables and cook for 4 to 5 minutes or until just tender.

Heat oil and fry garlic and ginger on low heat, stirring. Add ground spices and cook for a few minutes longer, then mix in fruit and vegetables. Put into a glass or china bowl and allow to cool, then bottle. Keeps well for weeks.

This popular South-East Asian pudding is a far cry from the sago pudding despised by children in boarding schools! Its local name, gula melaka, *means 'palm sugar'.*

GULA MELAKA

- *1 small stick cinnamon*
- *2 cups sago*
- *1 cup canned coconut milk*
- *2 pinches of salt*
- *250 g (8 oz) dark palm sugar or 1 cup canned palm syrup*
- *2 strips fresh or dried pandan leaves or few drops pandan essence*

In a large saucepan bring 8 to 10 cups water to a fast boil with cinnamon stick. Gradually add sago, stir and let boil for 7 minutes. Remove from heat, cover pan tightly and set aside for 10 minutes. (The sago grains will become clear when they have finished cooking in the stored heat.) Add cold water to the pan, stir sago and drain in a sieve. Shake so that water drains away. Discard cinnamon stick.

Turn sago into a bowl and stir in 2 tablespoons coconut milk and pinch of salt. (Milk takes away the grey appearance of the sago.) Transfer to individual serving dishes or moulds

or pour into 1 large mould. Chill until set.

Place palm sugar in a small saucepan with ½ cup water and pandan leaves or essence. Heat gently until sugar melts. Strain through a fine sieve into a small jug and allow to cool. Palm syrup does not need to be heated or diluted.

Dilute coconut milk with ¼ cup water, adding a pinch of salt—this brings out the flavour. Pour into another jug or serving bowl. Cover and leave at room temperature.

When ready to serve unmould sago and allow guests to help themselves to palm sugar syrup and coconut milk which are poured around and over each individual serving.

INDONESIA

A festive rice cone is perfect for a banquet. The gaily decorated yellow rice surrounded by accompaniments commemorates sacred mountains. The egg and chicken dishes can be made a day or two ahead—their flavours will improve with time. Prepare the rice last, reheating other dishes as necessary.

Serves 8 to 10

FRIED TAMARIND CHICKEN

- *1 tablespoon dried tamarind pulp*
- *4 cloves garlic*
- *2 teaspoons salt or to taste*
- *1½ teaspoons ground black pepper*
- *1 teaspoon palm sugar or black sugar*
- *3 teaspoons ground coriander*
- *1½ teaspoons ground cummin*
- *¾ teaspoon ground turmeric*
- *8 to 10 chicken drumsticks*
- *8 to 10 chicken thighs*
- *oil for frying*

Soak tamarind pulp in ½ cup hot water for 5 to 10 minutes. Squeeze to disperse pulp, strain through sieve to remove seeds and fibres and reserve liquid. Crush garlic with salt to a smooth paste and combine with pepper, sugar, coriander, cummin, turmeric and tamarind liquid. Rub over chicken pieces and leave for 1 hour, or cover and refrigerate overnight.

Heat sufficient oil in a large heavy frying pan to cover

base of pan. Drain chicken pieces on paper towels to remove excess moisture. Fry over medium heat, turning with tongs until golden brown. Pour off oil. Reduce heat, add any remaining marinade to pan, cover and cook for 10 minutes. Turn pieces halfway through. Uncover and cook until no liquid remains in pan. Drain and serve warm.

BEEF PATTIES WITH COCONUT

- *375 g (12 oz) minced beef*
- *1 teaspoon dried shrimp paste*
- *2 teaspoons crushed garlic*
- *2 teaspoons finely chopped lesser galangal in brine*
- *1 teaspoon salt*
- *½ teaspoon ground black pepper*
- *2 teaspoons ground coriander*
- *1 teaspoon ground cummin*
- *1 large egg, beaten*
- *2 cups fresh grated coconut*
- *or 1 cup desiccated coconut (see Note)*
- *oil for frying*

Put beef into a large bowl. Wrap shrimp paste in foil, press to flatten and roast under hot griller for about 2 minutes on each side. Dissolve in a little hot water. Add with garlic, galangal, salt, pepper and ground spices to the beaten egg and mix well. Pour over meat in bowl and mix, add coconut and mix again very thoroughly with hands. Form into small patties and shallow fry until crisp and golden brown. Drain on absorbent paper.

Note Grated coconut is now available in some Asian shops, often frozen but sometimes fresh. If using desiccated coconut, moisten with about 4 tablespoons water first, sprinkling it over and tossing it through.

STEAMED VEGETABLES

- *375 g (12 oz) fresh green beans*
- *6 carrots*
- *375 g (12 oz) bean sprouts*
- *1 small Chinese cabbage*
- *2 canned bamboo shoots*
- *1½ cups fresh grated or desiccated coconut*
- *1 teaspoon dried shrimp paste*
- *1 medium onion, chopped finely*
- *½ teaspoon sambal oelek*
- *1 teaspoon salt or to taste*
- *¼ cup lemon juice*

String beans if necessary and cut diagonally into slices. Peel carrots and cut into thin strips. Pinch tails off sprouts. Slice cabbage across into thin strips. Place in colander and rinse under cold water. Cut bamboo shoots into strips the same size as beans. If using desiccated coconut, place in a bowl and sprinkle with 3 tablespoons hot water; mix together with fingertips until evenly moistened.

Wrap shrimp paste in foil and heat under grill for

5 minutes. Add to coconut with onion, sambal oelek, salt and lemon juice. Mix thoroughly. Sprinkle coconut mixture through vegetables (reserving some mixture to garnish dish when served). Place vegetables in a steamer and cook for 5 to 8 minutes. Serve warm or at room temperature, sprinkled with reserved coconut.

A very hot dish—remember it is to be eaten sparingly.

Egg and Chilli Sambal

- *6 eggs*
- *¼ cup peanut oil*
- *2 medium onions, finely chopped*
- *2 cloves garlic, finely chopped*
- *2 teaspoons finely chopped galangal*
- *1 teaspoon dried shrimp paste*
- *1 tablespoon sambal oelek or crushed red chillies*
- *1 teaspoon salt*
- *1 tablespoon brown sugar*
- *1 cup canned coconut milk*
- *lemon juice to taste*

Hard-boil eggs. Heat oil and fry onions, garlic and galangal gently in a heavy pan until onion is soft and golden. Add shrimp paste and sambal oelek and fry for a few seconds, crushing shrimp paste with the back of a spoon. Add salt, brown sugar, coconut milk mixed with 1 cup water, and lemon juice. Simmer gently, stirring constantly, until thick and oily looking. Shell and halve eggs and add to pan, spooning sauce over them. Serve hot or at room temperature.

Shrimp wafers come in a variety of shapes, sizes and colours. Those with the best and most distinctive shrimp flavour are the large, roughly oblong, salmon-pink variety. Krupuk are based on a starch and ground shrimp mixture. When deep-fried in oil they become light, crisp and twice their original size.

KRUPUK

- *2 cups peanut oil for deep-frying*
- *12–16 large krupuk or 30 small ones*
- *melinjo crackers, optional*

Heat oil in wok or deep frying pan until a blue haze shimmers over surface. Test with a small piece first and if the wafer swells within 2 or 3 seconds of being dropped in, temperature is correct. If it sinks to the bottom of the oil and takes time to swell, krupuk will be tough and leathery instead of crisp. If it is too hot they will brown too quickly.

Fry large krupuk one at a time (if your pan is too small, break them in half before frying). Melinjo crackers can be fried a few at a time. Drain on absorbent paper. Serve fairly quickly, or cool thoroughly before storing in an airtight container.

Note Sometimes, in humid conditions, krupuk absorb moisture and do not puff as they should. A good precaution is to dry them out in a very slow oven, spread in a single layer on a baking tray. Cool before frying.

A hot, crisp accompaniment to arrange in little heaps around the rice cone.

CHILLI PEANUTS

- 2 cups raw peanuts
- 1 cup oil for frying
- 2 teaspoons crushed garlic
- 1 tablespoon sambal oelek or finely chopped fresh red chillies
- 3 tablespoons desiccated coconut
- 1 teaspoon salt, or to taste

In a wok, fry peanuts in oil until golden brown. Lift out with a slotted spoon and drain on paper towel. Pour off all but 2 tablespoons of oil and, on low heat, fry garlic, stirring, until golden. Add sambal and fry for 1 minute then add coconut and salt and fry, stirring, for a further minute. Return peanuts to wok and continue to stir-fry just until nuts are well mixed with chilli. Serve at room temperature.

Rice Cone

- 1 kg (2 lb) long grain rice
- ¼ cup oil
- 2 large onions, sliced finely
- 3 cloves garlic, chopped finely
- 4 cups canned coconut milk
- 4 teaspoons salt or to taste
- 2 teaspoons ground turmeric
- 3 daun salam or 6 curry leaves
- banana leaves for serving
- 6 small seedless cucumbers
- fresh red chillies
- fresh green chillies

Wash rice and leave to drain for at least 1 hour. Heat oil in a large saucepan which has a well-fitting lid (alternatively place a sheet of foil between pan and lid to make a good seal). Fry onions and garlic over low heat until soft and golden, stir frequently. Add rice and fry for 2 minutes, then add coconut milk mixed with 4 cups water, salt, turmeric and leaves. Bring to boil, stirring with a long-handled spoon. As soon as liquid comes to boil, turn heat low, cover tightly and allow to steam for 20 minutes. Remove cover and, with a fork, quickly stir in any coconut milk that remains unabsorbed around edge of rice. Replace lid and leave on same low heat for a further 3 minutes. Turn off heat, uncover and allow steam to escape and rice to cool slightly. Remove leaves.

Gently fork rice onto a large serving platter or a tray lined, if possible, with well-washed banana leaves. Shape rice into a cone, pressing firmly into shape. In Indonesia they mould it by pressing it into a cone-shaped basket and turning it out—you might try using a large Chinois if you have one.

Wash cucumbers and score skin lengthwise with a fork. Cut across into very thin slices. Reserve 1 red chilli and cut others into thin diagonal slices, removing seeds. With reserved chilli, make a flower by cutting off stem end and slicing chilli several times with the point of a sharp knife 2.5 cm (1 in) from tip to cut end at the stem. Place in iced water to curl. Surround cone with accompanying dishes and decorate with chillies and cucumber.

Coconut Icecream

- *1 teaspoon unflavoured gelatine*
- *¾ cup sugar*
- *400 mL can coconut milk*
- *½ teaspoon salt*
- *toasted shredded coconut*

Sprinkle gelatine over ¼ cup water and set aside for gelatine to soften. Combine sugar with 1½ cups water in a saucepan and stir over medium heat until sugar dissolves. Bring to boil, remove from heat and stir in gelatine until it dissolves. Stir in coconut milk and salt. Chill, then freeze in an icecream churn. If a churn is not available, still-freeze icecream, stirring two to three times during the freezing. Alternatively, freeze mixture until solid, then break up into chunks and purée in a food processor (using the steel blade) until smooth but not melted. Return to freezer in covered container. Press a piece of freezer plastic directly onto the surface of icecream to prevent ice crystals forming. Serve topped with toasted coconut.

THAILAND

MENU 1

Because of the immense popularity of Thai food, I have put together two menus, each of which serves 6 to 8 people. If you are planning to entertain 12 people, put both both menus together and have a greater variety of dishes instead of increasing quantities of either menu—that is how it would be done in Thailand. If joining menus, serve Galloping Horses and Deep Fried Crispy Noodles as appetisers, followed by the soup (increase this recipe to yield ¾ cup (6 oz) soup for each serving). Everything else can be served at once with Steamed Rice (see p. 44). Only the rice should be doubled— 1 kg (2 lb) rice cooked in 2 L (8 cups) of water.

A delicious and unusual appetiser consisting of a savoury pork and peanut mixture used as a topping for fresh fruit.

GALLOPING HORSES

- 375 g (12 oz) minced pork
- 2 tablespoons oil
- 2 teaspoons finely chopped garlic
- 2 teaspoons finely chopped coriander roots
- 3 tablespoons crushed roasted peanuts
- 2 fresh red chillies, seeded
- 2 tablespoons fish sauce
- ¼ teaspoon black pepper
- 3 tablespoons palm or brown sugar
- oil for frying
- mandarin segments or fresh pineapple slices
- coriander leaves

Place pork mince in a bowl. Heat 2 tablespoons oil and fry garlic and coriander roots over low heat until soft and golden. Add to pork. Then add peanuts and 1 chilli, finely chopped, fish sauce, pepper and sugar. Mix well and form into about 30 small balls, flattening each ball slightly. Pour just enough oil into a heavy frying pan to cover base. Fry pork patties over medium low heat until well browned on one side, then fry other side. Drain on paper towel and allow to cool.

Remove all traces of white pith from mandarins but leave fine membrane. Cut each segment open down back and lay resulting circles on a serving dish. If using pineapple, cut thin slices into bite-sized pieces. Place pork patties on fruit and garnish with small pieces of sliced chilli and coriander leaves.

RED CURRY OF BEEF

- *1.5 kg (3 lb) lean stewing steak*
- *4 cups canned coconut milk*
- *4 tablespoons Red Curry Paste (see p. 52)*
- *6 fresh or dried kaffir lime leaves*
- *2 or 3 tablespoons fish sauce to taste*
- *2 fresh red chillies, seeded and sliced*

- *1 tablespoon palm or brown sugar*
  - *½ cup fresh basil leaves*

Trim steak and cut into cubes. Heat 1½ cups coconut milk in a large saucepan, stirring, until it comes to the boil. Cook over low heat until milk thickens and looks oily. Add Red Curry Paste and fry for about 5 minutes, stirring constantly. When ready, curry paste will smell cooked and oil will start to separate from mixture.

Add beef and stir well, then add remaining coconut milk with 2 cups water and all remaining ingredients. Stir until mixture returns to boil, then lower heat and simmer until beef is tender. If liquid seems to be cooking away before beef is ready, add a little hot water and stir. There should be plenty of gravy with this dish—and it should be rich and red. Stir in palm sugar and basil leaves and serve with rice and accompaniments.

Traditionally made with underripe mangoes, tart green apples may be substituted if mangoes are not obtainable.

MANGO OR APPLE SALAD

- *4 underripe mangoes or green cooking apples*
  - *½ teaspoon salt or to taste*
  - *1½ tablespoons peanut oil*
  - *5 cloves garlic, thinly sliced*
    - *8 spring onions, sliced*
  - *250 g (8 oz) pork fillet, shredded*
  - *1 tablespoon dried prawn powder*
    - *1 tablespoon fish sauce*
  - *3 tablespoons roasted peanuts, crushed*
    - *1 tablespoon brown sugar*
    - *finely sliced red chillies*

Peel mangoes and cut flesh away from stones in thin slices. (Or peel and core apples and slice thinly.) Place in a large

oowl and sprinkle with salt. Heat oil and fry garlic and spring onions separately; remove with a slotted spoon and set aside. (Be careful not to let the garlic burn as it cooks very quickly.) In the same pan, quickly stir-fry pork until brown; stir in prawn powder, fish sauce, peanuts and sugar. Remove from heat. Just before serving, mix cooked ingredients into fruit in bowl and sprinkle with sliced chillies.

Note You may find ready-fried shallots and dried garlic in Asian supermarkets—this saves a lot of effort.

A pungent accompaniment which will give you the real flavour of Thailand although its taste is an acquired one.

Shrimp Paste Sambal

- 2 teaspoons dried shrimp paste
- 4 tablespoons finely chopped onion
- 1 tablespoon finely chopped garlic
- 4 tablespoons dried prawn powder
- ¼ cup lime or lemon juice
- 1 tablespoon palm or brown sugar
- fish sauce to taste
- 1 teaspoon finely shredded lime or lemon rind
- few thin slices fresh red chilli

Make a flat cake from dried shrimp paste and wrap entirely in foil. Place under hot griller and roast for 4 to 5 minutes on each side. Leave to cool. Pound shrimp paste with onion, garlic, and prawn powder in a mortar and pestle, adding lime or lemon juice gradually to work into a paste. Add sugar and fish sauce and mix well. Press into a small bowl and garnish with shredded rind and slices of chilli. Serve with raw vegetables for dipping.

Jasmine rice (most commonly used in Thailand) has a faint, delightful perfume which occurs naturally.

Steamed Rice

- 500 g (1 lb) jasmine or other long grain rice

Bring rice and 3½ cups water to boil in a heavy pan with a well-fitting lid. When water is bubbling, put lid on pan, turn heat down low and cook for 15 minutes. Do not uncover pan at all during this time. When cooking is complete, lift lid and let steam escape for a few minutes, then cover and keep warm until required.

Popularly known as Tuptim Grob, Tuptim is the Thai word meaning 'rubies' or 'pomegranate' and certainly the little red coloured pieces of tapioca-coated water chestnut resemble the jewel-like fruit. Grob means 'crisp', 'crunchy', which describes the texture.

WATER CHESTNUT SWEET

- *1½ cups sugar*
- *1 x 400 g (14 oz) can water chestnuts*
- *red food colouring*
- *few drops jasmine essence*
- *1½ cups tapioca flour*
- *1 cup canned coconut milk*
- *pinch salt*
- *crushed ice*

Mix sugar with 1½ cups water in a saucepan and heat, stirring until sugar dissolves. Cool and set aside.

Drain water chestnuts, rinse in cold water and cut each one into 3 one way and then the other, to give 9 pieces, roughly equal in size. Put into a bowl with just enough water to cover, and add red colouring to water. The colour should be fairly strong. Let soak for 15 minutes or until pieces of water chestnut absorb sufficient colour to make them bright red.

Spread tapioca flour on a sheet of greaseproof paper. When chestnuts have absorbed a fair amount of colour, drain in a sieve and toss to coat in tapioca flour. Bring a saucepan of water to boil. Gently shake coloured water chestnuts in a sieve to remove excess flour. Drop into water and cook until pieces rise to surface. Lift out on perforated spoon and plunge immediately into iced water.

To serve, pour about ¼ cup of syrup into each serving bowl. Carefully add some water chestnuts. Mix coconut milk with 1 cup cold water and a pinch of salt. Spoon a little into each bowl and add some crushed ice.

THAILAND

MENU 2

A popular Thai soup rich with creamy coconut milk and flavoured with fragrant herbs.

CHICKEN AND GALANGAL SOUP

- *1.5 kg (3 lb) chicken pieces*
- *3 cups canned coconut milk*
- *8 slices galangal, fresh, dried or in brine*
- *1 teaspoon black peppercorns*
- *1 tablespoon fresh coriander roots, crushed*
- *4 stalks lemon grass, thinly sliced*
- *4 fresh green chillies*
- *1½ teaspoons salt, or to taste*
- *8 kaffir lime leaves, fresh, frozen or dried*
- *2 tablespoons fish sauce*
- *⅓ cup fresh lime juice*
- *½ cup chopped fresh coriander leaves*

Place chicken in a saucepan with 1½ cups of coconut milk mixed with 2½ cups water. Add galangal, pepper, coriander roots, lemon grass, whole chillies, salt and lime leaves.

Bring to boil over low heat and simmer, uncovered, until chicken is tender, stirring occasionally. Discard chicken bones and skin, cut meat into bite-size pieces and return to pan. Add remaining coconut milk and stir constantly until mixture returns to boil. Remove from heat and stir in fish sauce and lime juice. Serve sprinkled with chopped coriander leaves.

DEEP-FRIED CRISPY NOODLES

- 250 g (8 oz) rice vermicelli
- 3 cups peanut oil for frying
- 250 g (8 oz) firm bean curd, finely diced
- 250 g (8 oz) finely minced pork
- 375 g (12 oz) raw prawns, shelled, deveined and chopped
- ½ teaspoon ground black pepper
- ½ teaspoon salt
- 4 tablespoons white wine vinegar
- 3 tablespoons sugar
- 3 tablespoons fish sauce
- 2 eggs, beaten
- 2 whole bulbs pickled garlic, sliced
- 3 or 4 finely sliced red chillies
- 1 cup fresh coriander leaves

Dip rice vermicelli briefly in cold water, shake off excess and leave near an open window to dry for at least 30 minutes. Separate into small handfuls.

Heat oil in a wok or deep frying pan until a light blue smoke rises from surface. Test heat with a few strands of vermicelli; they should puff up and float immediately. If not, wait until oil is hot enough, otherwise they will be tough and leathery. Cook a handful at a time, scooping them out as soon as they turn pale golden. Drain well on several sheets of paper towel. Cool completely. If preparing ahead, store airtight.

Deep fry diced bean curd till golden. Drain. Pour off oil, leaving ¼ cup. Add pork to wok and stir fry constantly until colour changes. Add prawns, fry until no longer transparent, then add pepper and salt. Stir vinegar, sugar and fish sauce together until sugar dissolves. Add to wok. When mixture boils add beaten eggs and keep stirring until egg is set and firm. This recipe can be prepared ahead to this stage, removed from wok and refrigerated, then heated through before serving.

To serve, combine fried vermicelli with heated mixture. Scatter pickled garlic slices, chillies and coriander leaves over top to garnish. It is absolutely imperative that this dish should be served immediately it is combined, or noodles will lose their delightful crispness.

MINCED BEEF SALAD

- 4 large dried red chillies
- 3 tablespoons peanut oil
- 4 tablespoons roasted rice powder (see Note)
- 750 g (1½ lb) premium quality minced beef
- ½ cup lime juice
- 2 stalks lemon grass, very finely sliced
  or finely grated rind of 1 lemon
- ½ cup chopped spring onions
- ½ cup chopped fresh mint leaves
- 3 tablespoons fish sauce, or to taste
- Asian or coral lettuce leaves
- mint sprigs
- lime wedges
- slices of fresh chilli

Fry chillies in hot oil until they are almost black—about 2 minutes. Drain on paper towel. When cool and crisp, chop finely—they will almost form a powder. Mix this with roasted rice powder. Poach beef in a small amount of boiling water just until colour changes from red to pink. Drain and place

in a bowl. Add chilli mixture and remaining ingredients, combining thoroughly.

Arrange beef mixture on washed and dried lettuce leaves and garnish with mint sprigs, lime wedges and chilli slices.

Note   If you are unable to purchase ready roasted and ground rice powder, you can make it yourself—the flavour is essential to this dish. Roast ½ cup raw rice in a dry pan over medium heat and stir constantly until grains are deep golden brown. Pound in a mortar and pestle until finely powdered.

Green Curry of Fish

- 1 kg (2 lb) firm white fish cutlets or fillets
- 2½ cups canned coconut milk
- 4 tablespoons Green Curry Paste (see p. 52)
- 6 to 8 kaffir lime leaves, fresh, frozen or dried
- 1 teaspoon salt or to taste
- 2 tablespoons fish sauce
- 4 tablespoons finely chopped fresh basil leaves
- 2 to 3 green chillies, seeded and chopped

Wash fish and dry on paper towels. Mix coconut milk with Green Curry Paste in a large wok and bring to boil, stirring constantly. Add lime leaves, salt and fish sauce, reduce heat and simmer for 15 minutes. Add fish and 1½ cups water and simmer until fish is cooked through—about 15 minutes. Add chillies and basil and simmer a few minutes longer.

STUFFED EGGS

- *6 large eggs*
- *250 g (8 oz) chopped raw prawns*
- *meat of 1 cooked crab*
- *125 g (4 oz) chopped cooked pork*
- *1 teaspoon red or green curry paste*
- *½ teaspoon ground black pepper*
- *½ teaspoon salt or to taste*
- *1½ tablespoons fish sauce*
- *1 to 2 tablespoons canned coconut milk*
- *½ cup plain flour*
- *2 teaspoons oil*

Boil eggs for 10 to 12 minutes, stirring water gently for first few minutes of cooking so yolks are centred. When cooked, run cold water into pan to cool eggs quickly. Shell eggs and cut in halves lengthwise.

Scoop yolks into a bowl and mash thoroughly with a fork. Add prawns, crab meat and pork, coriander leaves, pepper, salt and fish sauce. Mix well, then add sufficient coconut milk to bind mixture together. Do not let it get too moist.

Mix flour with ½ cup tepid water, adding oil and a pinch of salt. Beat with a wooden spoon until a smooth batter is formed.

Divide egg mixture into 8 equal portions and fill egg whites, rounding filling so it simulates a whole egg. Dip in batter and deep-fry in hot oil for 3 minutes or until golden brown. Drain on absorbent paper and serve warm or cold.

Thai Curry Pastes

Red Curry Paste
Makes about 1 cup

- 10 large or small fresh red chillies
- 2 cups chopped onions
- 1 teaspoon black peppercorns
- 2 teaspoons ground cummin
- 1 tablespoon ground coriander
- 2 tablespoons chopped fresh coriander root
- 1 teaspoon salt
- 1 stem lemon grass, finely sliced
 or 2 teaspoons chopped lemon rind
- 2 tablespoons chopped galangal in brine
- 1 tablespoon chopped garlic
- 2 teaspoons dried shrimp paste
- 1 teaspoon turmeric

Remove stems and seeds from chillies. Place all ingredients in a blender. Blend until smooth, stopping frequently to push ingredients down with a spatula. If necessary, add a little water. Store in a clean, dry, airtight glass jar in refrigerator for a month, or wrap and freeze in portions of convenient size.

Green Curry Paste
Makes about 1 cup

- 8 large or small green chillies
- 1 large onion, chopped
- 1 tablespoon chopped garlic
- 1 cup chopped fresh coriander, including roots, stems and leaves
- ¼ cup finely sliced lemon grass, or thinly peeled rind of 1 lemon
- 2 tablespoons chopped galangal, fresh or bottled in brine
- 2 teaspoons ground coriander
- 1 teaspoon ground cummin
- 1 teaspoon black peppercorns
- 1 teaspoon ground turmeric
- 1 teaspoon dried shrimp paste
- ⅓ cup lime or lemon juice

Blend and store as for Red Curry Paste.

YOUNG COCONUT, CORN AND BASIL SEEDS

- *1 tablespoon basil seeds (see Note)*
- *1 x 400 g can young coconut in syrup*
- *⅓ cup white sugar*
- *1 cup drained canned corn kernels*
- *2 or 3 drops jasmine essence, optional*
- *crushed ice*

Soak basil seeds in 1 cup water for 10 minutes so they develop a translucent coat. Drain young coconut; reserve syrup and add enough water to make 3 cups. Add sugar and stir over low heat until sugar dissolves. Add corn kernels and simmer about 10 minutes. Cool.

Cut young coconut flesh into small diamond shapes. Combine all ingredients in a bowl. Put about ¼ cup crushed ice into each dessert dish and pour over a generous ladle of coconut, corn and basil seed mixture with some of the syrup.

Note   Basil (manglak) seeds may be bought from Asian grocery stores.

BURMA

Burmese food is not synonymous with banquets; most popular meals are one-dish affairs—a great-tasting soup or curry served with noodles or rice, and accompanied by a range of flavour-boosting ingredients such as chopped fresh coriander and spring onions, fried chillies and garlic, fish sauce or lime wedges.

However, on those special occasions when a grand meal is in order, the aim is to serve as many dishes as possible—seafood, poultry, beef, pork. It is not necessary to make great quantities of each dish, but because there are a lot of them, a spread such as I describe will feed many people. The mainstay of the meal is, as usual, rice. It may be plain steamed (see p. 44) or cooked in coconut milk. Curries and accompaniments are added according to your budget and the time you have to prepare the meal. At the end of the meal you should always serve clear tea and a digestive nibble based on fresh ginger. Sweets are optional.

Serves 8 to 10

COCONUT RICE

- *1 kg (2 lb) long grain rice*
- *2 x 400 mL cans coconut milk*
- *3 teaspoons salt*

Put rice into a large, heavy saucepan with a well-fitting lid. Add canned coconut milk mixed with 4 cups hot water and salt and bring to the boil. Stir once or twice, cover and turn heat very low. Cook without lifting lid for 20 minutes. Uncover and, if coconut milk has not been absorbed, stir lightly with a fork around edge of pan, replace lid and leave on very low heat for 5 or 10 minutes longer. Turn off heat. Serve hot.

PORK CURRY

- 3 cups chopped onion
- 1 whole bulb of garlic, peeled
- 1 cup peeled, coarsely chopped fresh ginger
- 2 kg (4 lb) boneless pork with some fat, cut into large cubes
- 2 teaspoons salt
- 2 tablespoons vinegar
- 2 teaspoons chilli powder
- ½ cup peanut oil
- ¼ cup sesame oil
- 1 teaspoon ground turmeric

Put chopped onion, cloves of garlic and chopped ginger into food processor and grind to a purée. Pour into a strainer set over a bowl and press out juices. Reserve solids left in strainer. Put juices into a saucepan with pork, salt, vinegar and chilli powder. Bring to boil, cover and simmer slowly for 1½ hours or until pork is half-tender.

In another heavy saucepan heat peanut and sesame oils and fry residue of onions, garlic and ginger, adding turmeric and stirring for about 25 minutes until mixture smells mellow, turns a reddish brown and oil starts to separate from the mass. Add pork and any liquid in pan and continue to cook until pork is so tender it can be cut with a spoon. Stir as cooking nears completion to ensure it does not stick to pan.

Beef and Pumpkin Curry

- 1 kg (2 lb) stewing steak
- 750 g (1½ lb) pumpkin
- 3 large onions, chopped
- 10 large cloves garlic, peeled
- 1 tablespoon chopped fresh ginger
- 1½ teaspoons ground turmeric
- 1 teaspoon chilli powder
- ⅓ cup peanut oil
- ⅓ cup sesame oil
- 2 teaspoons salt

Trim beef and cut into large cubes. Peel and dice pumpkin into similar size pieces. Purée onions, garlic and ginger in blender or food processor. Mix in turmeric and chilli powder. Heat both kinds of oil in a heavy pan and fry purée over low heat for about 20 minutes or until it smells mellow, turns a rich reddish brown and oil glistens around the edge. This is the most important step of any Burmese dish and shouldn't be hurried.

Add beef and stir until coated. Add 1 cup water, cover and simmer until beef is almost done. Add pumpkin, salt and if liquid has cooked away, a little more water. Stir well, cover and cook until beef and pumpkin are very tender.

Dry Prawn Relish

- 250 g (8 oz) dried shrimp
- 1 cup peanut oil
- 2 teaspoons dried shrimp paste
- 2 teaspoons chilli powder
- 1 teaspoon salt
- ⅓ cup vinegar
- 1 cup crisp-fried shallots (see Note)
- 2 tablespoons fried garlic slices

In a food processor chop dried shrimp almost to a floss. Heat oil in wok and fry ground shrimp on low heat until crisp and dry. Combine shrimp paste, chilli powder, salt and vinegar, pour over prawns and continue to stir and fry until almost crisp. Cool completely before stirring in shallots and garlic. Store relish in an airtight jar.

Note   Crisp fried shallots may be purchased from Asian stores.

PRAWN CURRY

- *1.5 kg (3 lb) fresh raw prawns*
- *2 large onions*
- *8 cloves garlic*
- *3 teaspoons grated fresh ginger*
- *1 teaspoon ground turmeric*
- *1 teaspoon chilli powder*
- *¼ cup corn oil*
- *¼ cup sesame oil*
- *1½ teaspoons salt*
- *¼ cup chopped coriander leaves*
- *¼ cup chopped spring onion greens*

Shell and devein prawns. Purée onions, garlic, ginger, add turmeric and chilli powder and cook as for Beef and Pumpkin Curry (see p. 56) in both kinds of oil. When sizzling and oily, add prawns and stir well, scatter most of the chopped coriander leaves over, cover and cook for 5 minutes or until prawns change colour. Remove from heat and stir in the rest of the coriander and all the spring onion leaves. Serve with rice.

Ginger Salad

- *125 g (4 oz) very tender ginger roots*
- *lime or lemon juice*
- *3 tablespoons corn or peanut oil*
- *1 tablespoon Oriental sesame oil*
- *2 tablespoons chopped garlic*
- *salt to taste*
- *3 tablespoons toasted sesame seeds*

Peel ginger and cut into thin slices. Cut slices into fine shreds. Put into a bowl, add lime or lemon juice to cover and leave for at least 1 hour or until ginger turns pink.

Heat both oils in a small frying pan and fry garlic over low heat, stirring, until it is just pale gold, then move from heat at once. Drain ginger from lime juice, add salt to taste and sprinkle with fried garlic and toasted sesame seeds. Serve in small individual bowls (like Chinese sauce dishes) to be eaten with the fingers as a digestive.

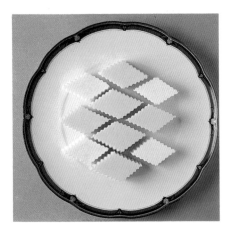

The transparent strands of this refined seaweed (known as agar-agar) resemble strips of crinkled cellophane.

SEAWEED JELLY
Makes about 18 pieces

- 7 g (¼ oz) agar-agar strands or 4 teaspoons agar-agar powder
- 2 cups canned coconut milk
- ½ cup sugar
- few drops rose essence or 1 tablespoon rose water
  (see Note, p. 6)
- food colouring, optional

Soak strands of agar-agar in cold water overnight—or for at least 1 hour. Drain and measure. You should have 1½ loosely packed cups. Place in saucepan with coconut milk mixed with 2 cups water and bring to boil, stirring constantly. Add sugar and continue to stir while simmering for 15 to 20 minutes, or until the strands are dissolved completely. (If using agar-agar powder, sprinkle powder over 2 cups water in saucepan and bring to boil. Add sugar and simmer, stirring, for 10 minutes. Remove from heat and stir in coconut milk.)

Flavour to taste with rose water or essence, add colour if you wish, pour into a dish rinsed out with cold water and allow to set. The jelly should be firm enough to pick up with the fingers. Cut into squares or diamond shapes.

VIETNAM

Serves 6 to 8

These crisply deep fried rolls would have to be one of the most popular items in Vietnamese cuisine. Go into any Vietnamese restaurant and you'll see, on every table, this favourite entree being happily consumed by Orientals and Occidentals alike.

FRIED PORK AND CRAB ROLLS
Makes about 30

- *50 g skein of bean starch noodles*
- *meat from 1 cooked crab*
- *300 g (10 oz) pork mince*
- *½ cup finely chopped spring onions*
- *½ teaspoon salt*
- *¼ teaspoon black pepper*
- *2 tablespoons fish sauce*
- *30 spring roll wrappers, 125 mm (5 inch) size*
- *oil for frying*
- *frilly Asian lettuce (or other pliable lettuce)*
- *sprigs of Vietnamese mint (polygonum odoratum), fresh coriander and mint*
- *strips of cucumber*

Soak bean starch noodles in hot water for 15 minutes, drain and cut into short lengths with a sharp knife. Put into a bowl and combine with crab meat, pork mince, spring onions, salt, pepper and fish sauce. Mix well.

Thaw spring roll pastry, carefully peel off individual sheets

and put a scant tablespoon of filling close to one end. Roll up, turning in the ends so filling is enclosed. When all rolls are made, heat oil in a wok and deep-fry in batches so as not to crowd the pan or lower heat of oil too much. Lift out with a slotted spoon when golden brown and drain on paper towels.

Serve a plate of lettuce leaves and sprigs of pungent herbs alongside rice paper rolls. Each person takes a roll, wraps it in a lettuce leaf and tucks in a sprig of mint, coriander or Vietnamese mint, and a strip of cucumber. It is then dipped and eaten (see below).

Dipping Sauce
- *⅓ cup fish sauce*
- *1 tablespoon vinegar*
- *1 clove garlic*
- *1 tablespoon sugar*
- *2 teaspoons finely chopped red chillies or sambal oelek*
- *juice and pulp of 1 lemon*
- *1 tablespoon fine shreds of carrot, optional*

Combine all ingredients, except carrots, with ¼ cup water, first crushing garlic to a smooth paste with some of the sugar. Cover and set aside. Before serving, stir in carrot shreds and give each person a small individual sauce bowl for dipping.

There are many vegetables which bear the name of Chinese cabbage, but the one to use here is the palest green, tightly closed variety with white leaf ribs. It has a delicate flavour and is known as wongah bak, Napa cabbage, celery cabbage, Peking or Tientsin cabbage!

CHICKEN AND CABBAGE SALAD

- half a Chinese cabbage
- 400 g chicken thigh fillets
- salt and pepper to taste
- 1 medium onion
- 2 tablespoons sugar
- 2 tablespoons fish sauce
- 3 tablespoons lime juice
- 1 tablespoon white wine vinegar
- ½ cup chopped mint or Vietnamese mint
- ¼ cup chopped coriander

Cut cabbage in halves again lengthwise, wash in cold water and shake out all water. Place cut surface down on a wooden board and, with a sharp knife, cut across into very thin slices. Put sliced cabbage into a bowl, cover with plastic wrap and chill.

Put fillets into a pan with just enough water to cover, add salt and pepper to taste. Bring to a slow simmer and cook, covered, until done. Do not overcook. Allow to cool in liquid.

Peel onion, halve lengthwise and slice very thinly crosswise. Sprinkle onion with ½ teaspoon of salt, leave for 30 minutes then rinse under cold water, squeezing out juices. Add half the sugar and mix. In another bowl, combine remaining sugar, fish sauce, lime juice and vinegar. Slice cooled chicken finely and toss with cabbage.

Just before serving, add onion, combined dressing ingredients, mint and coriander and toss well.

Note Vietnamese mint (rau ram) is sold in many Asian greengrocers and at growers markets. If you are buying a plant at a nursery, ask for *polygonum odoratum*.

Beef with Crushed Sesame

- *750 g (1½ lb) rump or fillet steak*
  - *4 tablespoons peanut oil*
  - *12 spring onions, sliced*
  - *2 tablespoons fish sauce*
  - *1 teaspoon salt or to taste*
  - *2 cloves garlic, finely chopped*
- *⅔ cup sesame seeds, toasted and crushed*

Cut beef into very thin slices—about 5 cm (2 in) long. Add 2 tablespoons oil to wok and stir-fry beef quickly over high heat—only about 1 minute. Remove from wok while meat is still pink. Repeat with remaining oil and meat. Add spring onions to oil remaining in wok and stir fry for about 1 minute. Add fish sauce and salt. Stir in garlic, frying for 1 more minute, then return beef to wok and stir-fry for 1 minute. Add sesame seeds and mix well. Serve hot with Pot Roasted Rice (see below).

Pot Roasted Rice

- *500 g (1 lb) short or medium grain rice*
  - *2 tablespoons peanut oil*

Wash rice and drain for 30 minutes or until dry. Heat oil in a heavy saucepan. Fry rice, stirring gently with a slotted metal spoon for 10 to 15 minutes or until rice becomes opaque and turns golden. Add 2 cups hot water, bring to boil then reduce heat to very low. Cover with a tight-fitting lid (or place a sheet of foil under lid to make a good seal) and cook for 20 minutes.

Sweet Pork

- 1.25 kg (2½ lb) pork belly or loin
- 2 tablespoons peanut oil
- 3 spring onions, finely chopped
- 2 teaspoons sugar
- ¼ teaspoon ground black pepper
- ½ teaspoon salt
- 2 tablespoons fish sauce

Cut pork into large cubes, leaving any fat as this adds to the delicious flavour of the dish. Heat oil in a wok and fry spring onions and pork, stirring, until pork is brown. Stir in sugar, salt and pepper, add 4 cups boiling water and simmer, uncovered, for 1 hour. Add fish sauce and continue simmering until liquid has almost evaporated. Stir frequently as liquid reduces so that pork does not burn but becomes glazed and caramelised.

THE PHILIPPINES

In addition to its Malay and Chinese heritage, the cuisine of the Philippines is greatly influenced by Spanish conquerors who came in the sixteenth century and stayed four hundred years.

Serves 6 to 8

A Philippine version of spring rolls which may be fried (like Chinese spring rolls) or fresh (popular in Thailand and Laos). For the fried version they should be wrapped in spring roll pastry. With fresh lumpia, the filling is enclosed first in a lettuce leaf and then in rice paper which has been briefly dipped in water to make it pliable. By the way, this is Asian rice paper, not the western kind which is used to line baking tins or wrap nougat and is more like a wafer in texture.

LUMPIA
Makes 12–16

- 2 tablespoons oil
- 1 tablespoon annatto seeds, optional
- 2 teaspoons finely chopped garlic
- 1 cup green beans, sliced diagonally
- 2 cups cooked, diced chicken
- 1 cup cooked pork in fine strips
- 1 cup small cooked prawns, shelled
- 1 cup finely diced water chestnuts
- 2 cups finely sliced Chinese cabbage (wongah bak)
- ½ cup finely sliced spring onions
- 1 tablespoon light soy sauce
- salt and pepper to taste
- 12 to 16 cos lettuce leaves
- 12 to 16 round rice paper sheets

Heat oil and fry annatto seeds over low heat, stirring, until oil is bright orange in colour. Remove seeds with a slotted spoon, and discard. In coloured and flavoured oil, cook garlic gently for a few seconds, then add sliced beans and stir-fry for 3 minutes or until tender but still crisp. Allow beans to cool. Add meat, vegetables (excluding lettuce), sauce and seasonings and toss well. Taste and adjust seasonings.

Dip a sheet of rice paper into lukewarm water for a few seconds to make it pliable. Place it on the work surface. Lay a cos lettuce leaf on rice paper and place a portion of filling on leaf. Roll it up so that one end is enclosed, with leaf showing at other end. Serve accompanied by Dipping Sauce.

Dipping Sauce

- *1 clove garlic*
- *3 tablespoons sugar*
- *1 cup clear chicken stock*
- *3 tablespoons light soy sauce*
- *2 tablespoons white wine or cider vinegar*
- *2 tablespoons tomato sauce*
- *2 tablespoons cornflour*

Crush garlic with sugar and combine with all other ingredients except cornflour. Bring to boil. Mix cornflour with a little cold water to a smooth cream, stir into mixture until it boils and thickens. Pour into a bowl and serve.

Pork Adobo

- 1 kg (2 lb) pork loin or forequarter chops
- 10 cloves garlic, crushed
- ½ cup white wine vinegar
- 2 tablespoons light soy sauce
- 2 bay leaves
- ½ teaspoon ground black pepper
- oil for frying
- tomato wedges and parsley for garnish

Cut pork into smaller serving pieces. Place pork and remaining ingredients (except oil) in a bowl and marinate for 1 hour. Transfer to a heavy saucepan, add 1 cup water and bring to boil then reduce heat and simmer until tender. Remove pork from pan and boil liquid over high heat until reduced and thickened. Strain into small bowl, and when it settles, spoon fat from top into a large frying pan. (Keep remaining sauce warm.) Add sufficient oil to pan so that base is covered with 5 mm (¼ in) fat. Fry pork until brown and crisp all over. Arrange on a heated serving plate and pour reserved sauce over. Garnish and serve with Steamed Rice (see p. 44).

Pawpaw Salad

- 1 large ripe, yet firm pawpaw
- 1 medium ripe pineapple
- 3 spring onions, finely sliced
- 1 green apple, peeled and diced
- ¾ cup thinly sliced celery
- ¾ cup good quality mayonnaise
- salt and pepper to taste

Cut pawpaw in halves, peel and scoop out seeds. Cut flesh into dice. Peel pineapple and cut into dice. Place in serving bowl; add remaining ingredients and gently mix together. Cover and chill before serving.

FLAN (CARAMEL CUSTARD)

- ½ cup sugar
- 4 large eggs
- 2 egg yolks
- ½ cup caster sugar
- 2 cups hot milk
- 1 cup evaporated milk
- 2 teaspoons vanilla

Mix sugar with ¼ cup water in a small heavy saucepan; heat without stirring until a deep golden brown. Pour immediately into a 6 cup ovenproof mould. Using oven mitts, rotate mould to coat base and sides with caramel.

Beat eggs and egg yolks together in a large bowl until foaming. Add caster sugar and beat until dissolved. Stir in hot milk gradually. Add evaporated milk and vanilla. Strain into caramel-lined mould. Stand mould in a baking tin and pour boiling water around to come half way up side of mould. Bake in oven at 150°C (300°F) for 35 to 45 minutes, or until a knife inserted in centre of custard comes out clean. Remove from oven and cool. When cold, cover and refrigerate for 2 days. Run a knife around edge. Invert a chilled serving plate over mould then, holding both together firmly, turn over so that custard slips onto plate. Serve chilled.

KOREA

Serves 6 to 8

Ideal for outdoor entertaining since the main dish is cooked on a barbecue. Except for the soup, serve all dishes with Steamed Rice (see p. 44)

DUMPLING SOUP

- *2 tablespoons oil*
- *185 g (6 oz) pork mince*
- *185 g (6 oz) lean beef mince*
- *250 g (8 oz) fresh bean sprouts*
- *half a small white Chinese cabbage*
- *1 x 300 g pack soft tofu*
- *3 spring onions, chopped finely*
- *2 tablespoons toasted, crushed sesame seeds*
- *2 cloves garlic, finely chopped*
- *1 teaspoon salt or to taste*
- *¼ teaspoon ground black pepper*
- *125 g (4 oz) wonton pastry squares*
- *omelette strips to garnish*
- *nori*
- *sesame oil*
- *extra salt to taste*
- *2 L strong beef stock*
- *6 large slices fresh ginger*
- *3 tablespoons light soy sauce*

Heat oil in wok and fry meats until colour changes. Add ½ cup water and simmer until liquid evaporates. Set aside. Boil bean sprouts in lightly salted water for 1 minute, drain and chop. Steam cabbage for 5 minutes, drain well and chop finely. Mash tofu. Mix all these ingredients with spring onions, sesame seeds, garlic, salt and pepper. Place a teaspoonful of mixture on each square of wonton pastry, dampen edges with water and press together to form a triangle. Place on a tray, not touching. Cover with plastic wrap and refrigerate.

Prepare omelette strips for garnish and set aside. Brush a sheet of nori liberally with sesame oil and sprinkle salt on one side. Grill until toasted and crisp. Crumble and set aside.

Put stock in a large saucepan and bring to boil with ginger, soy sauce and salt to taste. Drop in dumplings a few at a time, making sure they do not stick together. It may be necessary to cook them in batches. Simmer for 10 minutes or until dumplings are cooked and rise to surface. Remove ginger and serve soup and dumplings immediately in small bowls garnished with omelette strips and crumbled nori.

Note Dumplings may be made 2 to 3 hours before they are required. If desired, they can be served as a tasty appetiser instead of in soup. Simply deep-fry in several batches, drain on paper towel and offer with Dipping Sauce (see below).

DIPPING SAUCE
- *¾ cup soy sauce*
- *3 tablespoons white wine vinegar*
- *3 tablespoons crushed, toasted sesame seeds*
- *2 tablespoons finely chopped spring onions*

Blend all ingredients together and pour into small sauce bowls.

FIERY BEEF

- *1 kg (2 lb) lean rump or fillet steak, in one piece*
- *¼ cup soy sauce*
- *2 tablespoons finely chopped spring onions*
- *1 teaspoon crushed garlic*
- *½ teaspoon finely grated fresh ginger*
- *2 teaspoons sugar*
- *¼ teaspoon black pepper*

- *1 tablespoon toasted, crushed sesame seeds*
  - *Sauce (see below)*

Partially freeze steak until firm—this will make it easier to slice. Cut steak into paper thin slices and then into bite-sized pieces. Mix remaining ingredients together with ¼ cup water in a large bowl. Add steak and leave to marinate, covered, for 3 hours or longer in refrigerator.

When ready to serve, grill steak briefly on an oiled grid placed over glowing coals on a barbecue. Serve accompanied by Sauce in small individual sauce bowls.

Sauce
- *1 small clove garlic*
  - *salt to taste*
- *2 teaspoons sugar*
- *3 tablespoons soy sauce*
- *2 teaspoons sesame oil*
- *2 tablespoons rice wine or dry sherry*
- *1 teaspoon toasted, ground sesame seeds*
- *2 teaspoons finely chopped spring onions*
  - *1 teaspoon chilli sauce*

Crush garlic to a fine paste with salt and sugar. Place in a small bowl and add remaining ingredients. Add 2 tablespoons water and stir together, mixing well.

One of Korea's national dishes, it is now possible to buy it in specialty Asian food stores and delicatessens. Ask for Kim Chi.

PICKLED CABBAGE

- *1 large white Chinese cabbage*
- *common salt or sea salt (not iodised)*
- *cayenne pepper*
- *6 spring onions, finely chopped*
- *1 tablespoon finely chopped garlic*
- *3 fresh red chillies, finely chopped*
- *1 tablespoon finely chopped fresh ginger*
- *2 cups dashi stock (see Note)*
- *2 teaspoons light soy sauce*

Cut base off cabbage and discard. Slice remainder lengthwise into 6 segments. Place on a tray and dry in sun for half a day. Cut each segment in halves crossways. Place in an earthenware pot alternately with good handfuls of salt and a sprinkling of cayenne pepper. Make several layers. Cover with a wooden board just small enough to fit inside pot so that it rests directly on the cabbage and weighs it down. Leave for 1 week then rinse cabbage thoroughly under cold running water and squeeze out as much moisture as possible. Slice across into 2.5 cm (1 in) sections and return to the rinsed out pot, this time layering with a mixture of chopped spring onions, garlic, chillies and ginger. Mix dashi stock with soy sauce and fill pot. Cover with waxed paper; replace lid and refrigerate. The pickle will be ready to eat after 4 or 5 days. (In cold weather this pickle does not require refrigeration, but when the weather is warm store in refrigerator for up to 3 weeks.)

Note Make up stock according to instructions on packet or bottle of dashi concentrate.

GREEN BEANS WITH PRAWNS

- 625 g (1¼ lb) small raw prawns
- 625 g (1¼ lb) green beans
- 2 tablespoons vegetable oil
- 1 tablespoon sesame oil
- 1 large onion, sliced thinly
- 4 tablespoons light soy sauce
- 1½ teaspoons sugar
- 1 tablespoon toasted, crushed sesame seeds

Shell and devein prawns and chop roughly. Trim beans and remove strings if necessary. Cut into thin diagonal slices. Heat oils in wok and stir-fry onion and prawns for 2 minutes; add beans and stir-fry for another 3 minutes. Add remaining ingredients, mixing well. Cover and simmer over low heat until beans are just tender—about 6 to 8 minutes. Do not overcook. Serve immediately.

CHINA

In family-style Chinese meals all the dishes are brought to the table at once; at restaurant banquets, however, each dish is presented separately, heightening anticipation and allowing each one to be appreciated on its own. A compromise is to serve Cloud Swallows first, followed by the Cold Lemon Chicken, then place a covered container of hot steamed rice on the table with the rest of the banquet dishes. Clear the table before presenting dessert.

Serves 6 to 8

Tiny savoury dumplings made with wonton wrappers which, when deep-fried, can be served as an appetiser. The picturesque name comes from the fact that with a bit of imagination the points of the pastry represent beak and wings of a little swallow.

CLOUD SWALLOWS
Makes about 40

- 6 dried shiitake (Chinese) mushrooms
- ¼ cup finely chopped canned bamboo shoots
- 375 g (12 oz) raw prawns
- 4 spring onions, finely chopped
- 250 g (8 oz) minced pork
- 1 teaspoon salt, or to taste
- 1 tablespoon light soy sauce
- 1 teaspoon sesame oil
- 250 g (8 oz) wonton wrappers
- peanut oil for frying

Place mushrooms in a bowl, add hot water to cover and soak for 30 minutes. Squeeze out excess moisture, cut off stems

and discard. Chop mushrooms finely. Peel and devein prawns, chop finely. Mix all chopped ingredients with minced pork, salt, soy sauce and sesame oil.

Place ½ teaspoonful of filling in the centre of each wonton wrapper, moisten edges of dough with water and fold to form a triangle with its points slightly overlapping; press together. Bring the two base ends of triangle together, dab with a little filling where they join and press to seal. When all are ready, deep fry (a few at a time) on medium heat until golden.

COLD LEMON CHICKEN

- 1 x 1.5 kg (3 lb) roasting chicken
- salt
- 2 spring onions
- 2 sprigs celery leaves
- few black peppercorns
- few sprigs fresh coriander
- 4 tablespoons Chinese lemon sauce
- 1 tablespoon light soy sauce
- ½ cup finely chopped chives
- 2 teaspoons finely grated fresh ginger

Wash chicken. Remove any fat from cavity and cut off and discard tail and wing tips. Wipe dry with paper towels, then rub salt over surface and inside cavity. Choose a saucepan just large enough to hold chicken. Add 2 L of water, spring onions, celery leaves, peppercorns, coriander and 2 teaspoons salt, or to taste. Bring to boil, then lower chicken into pan, breast downwards. Let water return to boil, then reduce heat so that it just simmers. Cover pan tightly and cook for 25 minutes. Remove from heat and leave chicken in liquid with pan still tightly covered for a further 45 minutes to finish cooking. Lift out and drain chicken (reserving stock for another use). Leave to cool.

Remove all skin and bones from cooled chicken and slice meat thinly. Arrange on a serving dish. Mix lemon sauce and soy sauce together and pour over chicken. Leave chicken to marinate in this mixture for at least 30 minutes. When ready to serve sprinkle with mixture of chopped chives and ginger.

BRAISED CRAB WITH GINGER

- 2 large cooked crabs
- 3 tablespoons peanut oil
- 2 cloves garlic, finely chopped
- 1 tablespoon finely shredded fresh ginger
- 2 tablespoons light soy sauce
- 2 tablespoons sherry
- 1 teaspoon Tabasco sauce, optional
- 2 teaspoons sugar
- 6 spring onions, finely sliced

Remove carapace (top shell). Discard fibrous tissue found under shell, and stomach bag. Rinse crabs, divide each into quarters. Separate claws from body and crack shells to allow flavours to penetrate.

Heat peanut oil in wok and over low heat fry garlic and ginger until soft and starting to change colour. Stir in soy, sherry,

Tabasco sauce (if a touch of heat is desired), sugar and ¼ cup water until sugar dissolves. When boiling put in crabs, cover and simmer 8 minutes, turning pieces over half way through. Sprinkle with spring onions, cover and cook 1 minute longer.

Note If using raw crabs, boil or fry on high heat until they change from blue or green to red. Do this before adding any other ingredients to oil. Then proceed with recipe as above.

HEAVENLY BRAISED VEGETABLES

- *18 dried shiitake (Chinese) mushrooms*
- *½ cup dried wood fungus*
- *2 x 230 g (7½ oz) cans sliced bamboo shoots*
- *1 x 425 g (15 oz) can young corn cobs*
- *2 tablespoons peanut oil*
- *2 tablespoons sesame oil*
- *4 tablespoons soy sauce*
- *2 tablespoons sugar*

Soak mushrooms in 2 cups very hot water for 30 minutes. Remove and discard stems, squeeze out excess moisture from caps. Reserve mushroom liquid. Soak wood fungus in water for 10 minutes, rinse and drain, then cut each piece in two. Drain and slice bamboo shoots thinly. Drain corn.

Heat oils in a wok and fry mushrooms over high heat, stirring all the time, until browned—about 5 minutes. Add remaining ingredients except fungus. Add reserved mushroom liquid, cover and simmer over low heat for 35 to 40 minutes. Add wood fungus and heat through.

HONEYED PORK WITH CHILLI

- *750 g (1½ lb) pork fillet*
- *2 teaspoons crushed garlic*
- *2 teaspoons finely grated fresh ginger*
- *1 teaspoon salt*
- *1 teaspoon five-spice powder*
- *2 tablespoons peanut oil*
- *3 cups sliced mustard cabbage*
- *1 teaspoon chilli bean sauce or Tabasco*
- *1 tablespoon honey*
- *1 tablespoon hoi sin sauce*
- *1 teaspoon cornflour*

Cut fillet into lengths which fit in the wok or frypan. Rub pork with combined garlic, ginger, salt and five-spice powder, cover and set aside for 30 minutes.

Heat 1 tablespoon peanut oil in a wok and stir-fry mustard cabbage for 1 minute or until colour intensifies. Move to a plate. Add remaining oil and when hot brown pork lightly all over, turning with tongs. Reduce heat and add honey and hoi sin sauce with ¼ cup water. Cover and simmer 15 minutes. Lift pork onto a board. Return mustard cabbage to wok, cover and cook in the sauce a few minutes before placing on serving dish. Cut pork into diagonal slices and arrange on top. Thicken sauce with cornflour mixed with a tablespoon of cold water, boil and spoon over pork.

ORIENTAL MELON WITH SWEET WONTONS

- *1 watermelon or honeydew melon*
- *1 can longans*
- *1 can mandarin segments*

Wash and dry melon, cut off top third, scallop edges. With melon baller scoop out flesh, discarding seeds. Put melon balls into a bowl with longans and mandarins and some syrup from cans. Cover and chill. Fill shell with fruits just before serving. Sweet wontons may be served alongside.

SWEET WONTONS
- *1½ cups chopped stoned dates*
- *½ cup finely chopped walnut kernels*
- *1 teaspoon finely grated orange or lemon rind*
- *squeeze of orange juice*
- *1 packet wonton pastry (60 squares)*
- *peanut oil for deep-frying*
- *icing sugar for dusting*

Mix dates with chopped nuts, grated rind and enough juice to moisten mixture. Form small cylinders, place one diagonally on each square of wonton pastry and roll up so filling is completely enclosed. Twist ends of pastry to seal. Fry a few at a time in deep, hot oil until golden brown. Remove with a slotted spoon and drain on paper towels. Sprinkle with icing sugar and serve.

JAPAN

Japanese cuisine exemplifies the saying: 'Less is more.' Instead of laden dishes and the groaning board, exquisitely presented small dishes are chosen according to the season of the year.

Serves 6

This dish is made with raw fish, and it is imperative that the fish be very fresh. Buy it on the day that it is being eaten and do not purchase any fish that has been frozen. You can use fish such as tuna, salmon, ocean trout, bream, moonfish, or other fish in season. A new departure is the addition of avocado.

SASHIMI

- *750 g (1½ lb) fresh fish fillets*
- *1 firm ripe avocado, peeled, quartered and sliced*
- *1½ tablespoons prepared wasabi (green horseradish)*
- *½ cup Japanese soy sauce*
- *½ cup mirin or dry sherry*

With a very sharp stainless-steel knife, cut each fillet into very thin slices. Arrange on a plate or tray. (Thin slices of some fish can be curled into flower shapes, tuna can be cut into small cubes, or slices may be arranged overlapping in a row.) Arrange avocado slices. Decorate with a few washed maple leaves or other non-poisonous leaves. Serve with small dishes of wasabi and of soy mixed with mirin or sherry. Each person mixes a small amount of wasabi into the soy to their own taste and dips a slice of fish or avocado in mixture before eating.

In Japan this custard is regarded as a soup and eaten with a spoon.
In summer the dish may be served cold.

STEAMED EGG CUSTARD WITH SEAFOOD

- *6 dried shiitake (Chinese) mushrooms*
- *3 tablespoons Japanese soy sauce*
- *1½ tablespoons sugar*
- *6 small prawns*
- *6 fresh oysters or scallops*
- *6 eggs*
- *3½ cups dashi stock (see Note)*
- *1½ teaspoons salt or to taste*
- *3 tablespoons sake, mirin or dry sherry*

Soak mushrooms in hot water 30 minutes. Cut off stems and discard. Simmer caps in a small saucepan with 1 cup soaking water, 1½ tablespoons of the soy sauce and sugar for 8 to 10 minutes. Shell and devein prawns.

Meanwhile, prepare custard. Beat eggs, then stir in all other ingredients, plus remaining 1½ tablespoons soy sauce.

In individual custard cups or ramekins (or use chawan mushi cups if you have them) place a mushroom, a prawn, and an oyster or scallop. Fill cups with custard mixture, carefully skimming off any bubbles from top of mixture. Place cups in a baking pan with hot water to come halfway up the sides. Bake in moderate oven for 15 minutes or until set. Serve hot or cold.

Note Make up dashi stock following instructions on packet or bottle of dashi concentrate.

MARINATED GRILLED CHICKEN

- *750 g (1½ lb) chicken thigh fillets*
- *6 tablespoons teriyaki barbecue sauce*
- *6 spring onions*

Trim all visible fat from chicken and cut into bite-size pieces of equal size. Marinate for 1 hour in teriyaki sauce, or in a mixture of 4 tablespoons Japanese soy sauce, 2 teaspoons sake and 2 teaspoons sugar.

Cut spring onions into short lengths and thread pieces of chicken and onion onto skewers. Cook over glowing coals or under a preheated griller until chicken is golden brown. Serve at once. Steamed rice may accompany chicken.

Note Soak bamboo skewers in cold water while preparing and marinating chicken to prevent burning.

A simple and refreshing lemon jelly.

AWAYUKI

- *1½ sticks kanten or 1 tablespoon agar-agar powder*
- *1 cup sugar*
- *¼ cup strained lemon juice*
- *2 egg whites*
- *strawberries to decorate*

If using kanten, break sticks into pieces and soak in 2 cups water for 30 minutes, then bring to boil and simmer until completely dissolved, stirring occasionally. If using agar-agar powder, sprinkle evenly on surface of 2 cups water in a saucepan and stir until it boils and dissolves. Add sugar and stir to dissolve. Remove from heat, stir in lemon juice.

Whisk egg whites in a clean, dry bowl until stiff. When lemon mixture is still slightly warm (it will set at room temperature), add it to the egg whites, mixing well. Pour into a mould or dish rinsed in cold water and leave to set. Or use individual dishes if preferred. Chill. Decorate with fanned strawberries.

Post script

Because this book aims to help you cope with those special occasions when there might be up to 12 people around your table, the recipes are on a somewhat grander scale than you would need for everyday cooking.

Love the ideas but don't want to cook for 12 people? Certainly it's all right to cut quantities, keeping proportions the same. But it doesn't always work the other way when increasing the number of portions. The general rule is that liquid is not increased in direct proportion to other ingredients. For example, if doubling the other ingredients, increase the liquid only by half.

Mixing and matching food

Some dishes go well with those from other countries, while others do not. As a guide, the flavours of Sri Lanka, Indonesia, Malaysia and Singapore are compatible but would not complement dishes from the Far East because their spiciness would overpower more subtle flavours.

Gently spiced and fragrant North Indian food is best appreciated by itself.

Thai food with its distinct combinations of herbs and spices is also best eaten on its own but can be eaten with Burmese food. Thailand and Burma share a border and, while the Burmese do not use as many herbs, the two countries use similar ingredients. Knowing how popular Thai food is, I have offered two menus; you can combine dishes from both according to your taste.

With its strong Spanish influence, Filipino food stands apart from other Asian regions. Japanese food is also totally individual. So savour them as such.

Good cooking and happy eating!

Glossary

You can find most of these ingredients in Asian stores and many are also sold in supermarkets, etc.

Agar-agar Seaweed, used for making jellies in Asian countries as it sets without refrigeration. It must be brought to the boil and completely dissolved. It has no flavour of its own. Easiest to use in its refined forms—powder, dried strands, or wide sticks.

Basil seeds The seeds of the small-leafed, lemon-scented basil (*ocimum canum*). Tiny, oval and brownish-black when dry, they develop a whitish, translucent coat when soaked in water for a few minutes. They are highly prized for having a cooling effect on the body.

Chillies Fresh chillies should be handled with care as the volatile oils can cause much discomfort. Small chillies are hotter than large ones. Wear gloves when handling. It is possible to buy fresh chopped chillies in jars which may be substituted, and also Sambal Oelek (Ulek) which is a mixture of fresh chillies and salt. Or there is Tabasco Pepper Sauce. Use 1 teaspoon in place of each hot chilli.

Coconut milk Since coconut milk is available in cans, it is quick and painless to use but brands differ in concentration. Very thick coconut milk will need to be diluted with twice as much water and very thin coconut milk can be used straight.

Galangal A rhizome resembling ginger; important in certain South-East Asian dishes. Available fresh, frozen, dried or sliced in brine.

Garam masala Essential in Indian dishes. Roast separately until fragrant—2 tablespoons coriander seeds, 1 tablespoon cummin seeds, 2 teaspoons whole black peppercorns, 1 teaspoon cardamom seeds (remove from pods), 2 cinnamon sticks and 10 whole cloves. Grind as finely as possible and mix in half a nutmeg, finely grated. Store airtight.

Gold leaf Gauze-thin sheets of beaten 23 carat gold used to decorate food on grand occasions. Purchase from Indian specialist shops or art suppliers. Pricey, quite edible, and rumoured to have aphrodisiac qualities.

Hoi sin sauce A thick, dark, sweet bean sauce mostly served as a condiment rather than being added to food.

Jaggery Another name for palm sugar when dry enough to be pressed into cakes. There are many grades of palm sugar, some dark as molasses and others almost white. The best flavour is obtained when the colour is somewhere in between, like *cafe au lait*.

Kanten Agar-agar in stick form the base of many desserts.

Kaffir lime leaves Essential in Thai cooking. Available fresh, frozen or dried.

Kalonji (nigella) A small black seed with distinctive flavour sold in Indian stores. No substitute.

Nori Laver seaweed, sold in thin sheets.

Palm sugar Obtained from various tropical palms, it has a distinct flavour but may be substituted by brown sugar.

Saffron Make sure you get true saffron, because there are imitations and nothing else has the same flavour. Expensive, but very little is needed and it keeps indefinitely. Best to buy the dried strands, or tiny packets of powdered saffron. There is no such thing as cheap saffron.

Sambal oelek (ulek) See chillies.

Shrimp, dried Important in South-East Asian cooking, both to simmer whole with soups and also to pulverise to a floss and cook with chilli for hot sambals.

Shrimp paste   Made from dried shrimp, this is powerful stuff but is used in tiny quantities. It makes a great difference in flavour. Sold in jars or blocks. Keeps indefinitely.

Soy sauce   There are many types. For best results, use the specified kind.

Silver leaf   Made from pure silver beaten incredibly thin, this is sold at Indian grocers where it is called 'varak' or at art supplies shops. It is edible. You only need a smidgin.

Tamarind   Fruit of a tropical tree, tamarind gives acidity to many dishes. It is sold dried, puréed or instant. The dried pulp has the truest flavour. Soak in hot water, dissolve pulp, strain. You can also spoon the purée from a jar or dissolve instant tamarind in hot water, but some of these are too acid or salty. Check strength before adding and adjust quantity accordingly.

Talsi   Indian name for basil seeds.

Vietnamese mint   Actually not a mint at all, but *polygonum odoratum*. Has a tingly, faintly hot flavour. Available at Asian markets and some nurseries. Substitute mint.

Wasabi   Root of a riverside plant native to Japan, not really 'green horseradish', though it has come to be known as such because it has much the same effect on tear ducts and sinuses. It is always served (in minute amounts) with raw fish dishes such as sashimi and sushi.

Index